WILLIAM SHAKESPEARE:
THE TRAGEDY OF KING RICHARD II

THE TRAGEDY OF

KING RICHARD II

By WILLIAM SHAKESPEARE

DESIGN BY DANIEL HABERMAN
ILLUSTRATIONS BY ISADORE SELTZER

PUBLISHED BY
THE COMPOSING ROOM, INC.
FINCH, PRUYN & COMPANY, INC.
RAE PUBLISHING CO., INC.
A. HOROWITZ & SON

INTRODUCTION—*A pilgrim soul*

King Richard the Second, by William Shakespeare
is the ninth in a series of annual keepsakes prepared for the
friends of the publishers.

The Tragedy of King Richard the Second was completed in 1595,
and is the beginning of a tetralogy of history plays. In the character of
Richard, the poet may be seen groping for the ambivalence of
Hamlet and, in any event, this king has elicited more antithetical
comment than any of Shakespeare's characters.

As Richard had a poet's soul, it is only natural that poets should
rally to the King's aid: Walter Raleigh indicated that "it is difficult to
condemn Richard without taking sides against poetry"; and W. B. Yeats
felt that Richard failed "because he had certain qualities that are
uncommon in all ages"; and John Masefield noted that "the tragedy of the
sensitive soul, always acute, becomes terrible when that soul is
made king here by one of the accidents of life."

The first folio edition of 1623 was again used as a guide in the
preparation of this book. Once more the publishers are indebted to
Isadore Seltzer, whose illustrations reflect sensitive attention to the play,
and whose time is always generously given.

Scene: England and Wales, Circa 1400

PROLOGUE—*Raphael Holinshed*
From The Chronicles of 1587

It fell out that in this parliament holden at Shrewsbury, Henry, Duke of Hereford, accused Thomas Mowbray, Duke of Norfolk, of certain words which he should utter in talk had betwixt them, as they rode together lately before betwixt London and Brainford, sounding highly to the King's dishonor. And for further proof thereof, he presented a supplication to the King, wherein he appealed the Duke of Norfolk in field of battle for a traitor, false and disloyal to the King and enemy unto the realm. This supplication was read before both the dukes in presence of the King: which done, the Duke of Norfolk took upon him to answer it, declaring that whatsoever the Duke of Hereford had said against him other than well, he lied falsely like an untrue knight as he was. And when the King asked of the Duke of Hereford what he said to it, he, taking his hood off his head, said: "My sovereign lord, even as the supplication which I took you importeth, right so I say for truth, that Thomas Mowbray, Duke of Norfolk, is a traitor, false and disloyal to your royal majesty, your crown, and to all the states of your realm."

DRAMATIS PERSONAE

KING RICHARD II, *King of England*

EDMUND, *Duke of York, uncle to Richard*

JOHN OF GAUNT, *Duke of Lancaster, uncle to Richard*

HENRY BOLINGBROKE, *son to Gaunt, later King Henry IV*

DUKE OF AUMERLE, *son to York*

THOMAS MOWBRAY, *Duke of Norfolk*

EARL OF NORTHUMBERLAND, *father to "Hotspur"*

HARRY PERCY, *later "Hotspur"*

QUEEN ISABEL, *second wife to King Richard*

DUCHESS OF GLOUCESTER, *sister-in-law to Gaunt*

DUCHESS OF YORK, *mother to Aumerle*

EARLS OF SALISBURY, BERKELEY

LORDS ROSS, WILLOUGHBY, FITZWATER

SIRS BUSHY, BAGOT, GREEN, SCROOP, PIERCE

CHURCHMEN, LORD MARSHAL, LADIES AND OTHERS

ACT ONE

[Enter King Richard, John of Gaunt,
with other Nobles and Attendants]

Richard. Old John of Gaunt, time-honored Lancaster,
    Hast thou according to thy oath and band
    Brought hither Henry Hereford, thy bold son,
    Here to make good the boist'rous late appeal,
    Which then our leisure would not let us hear,
    Against the Duke of Norfolk, Thomas Mowbray?

Gaunt. I have, my liege.

Richard. Tell me, moreover, hast thou sounded him,
    If he appeal the Duke on ancient malice,
    Or worthily, as a good subject should,
    On some known ground of treachery in him?

Gaunt. As near as I could sift him on that argument,
    On some apparent danger seen in him
    Aimed at your Highness, no inveterate malice.

Richard.	Then call them to our presence: face to face,
	And frowning brow to brow, ourselves will hear
	The accuser and the accused freely speak.
	High-stomached are they both, and full of ire,
	In rage, deaf as the sea, hasty as fire.

[Enter Bolingbroke and Mowbray]

Bolingbroke.	Many years of happy days befall
	My gracious sovereign, my most loving liege!
Mowbray.	Each day still better other's happiness,
	Until the heavens envying earth's good hap,
	Add an immortal title to your crown!
Richard.	We thank you both; yet one but flatters us,
	As well appeareth by the cause you come,
	Namely to appeal each other of high treason.
	Cousin of Hereford, what dost thou object
	Against the Duke of Norfolk, Thomas Mowbray?

Bolingbroke.　First—heaven be the record to my speech!—

In the devotion of a subject's love,

Tend'ring the precious safety of my prince,

And free from other misbegotten hate,

Come I appellant to this princely presence.

Now, Thomas Mowbray, do I turn to thee,

And mark my greeting well: for what I speak,

My body shall make good upon this earth,

Or my divine soul answer it in heaven.

Thou art a traitor and a miscreant,

Too good to be so, and too bad to live;

Since the more fair and crystal is the sky,

The uglier seem the clouds that in it fly.

Once more, the more to aggravate the note,

With a foul traitor's name stuff I thy throat,

And wish—so please my sovereign—ere I move,

What my tongue speaks my right-drawn sword may prove.

Mowbray.   Let not my cold words here accuse my zeal:

     'Tis not the trial of a woman's war,

     The bitter clamor of two eager tongues,

     Can arbitrate this cause betwixt us twain;

     The blood is hot that must be cooled for this.

     Yet can I not of such tame patience boast,

     As to be hushed, and naught at all to say.

     First, the fair reverence of your Highness curbs me

     From giving reins and spurs to my free speech,

     Which else would post until it had returned

     These terms of treason doubled down his throat.

     Setting aside his high blood's royalty,

     And let him be no kinsman to my liege,

     I do defy him, and I spit at him,

     Call him a slanderous coward and a villain;

     Which to maintain, I would allow him odds,

     And meet him were I tied to run afoot

Even to the frozen ridges of the Alps,

Or any other ground inhabitable,

Where ever Englishman durst set his foot.

Meantime, let this defend my loyalty:

By all my hopes most falsely doth he lie.

Bolingbroke. Pale trembling coward, there I throw my gage,

Disclaiming here the kindred of the King,

And lay aside my high blood's royalty,

Which fear, not reverence, makes thee to except.

If guilty dread have left thee so much strength

As to take up mine honor's pawn, then stoop.

By that, and all the rites of knighthood else,

Will I make good against thee, arm to arm,

What I have spoke, or thou canst worse devise.

Mowbray.   I take it up; and by that sword I swear,

            Which gently laid my knighthood on my shoulder,

            I'll answer thee in any fair degree

            Or chivalrous design of knightly trial;

            And when I mount, alive may I not light,

            If I be traitor or unjustly fight.

Richard.   What doth our cousin lay to Mowbray's charge?

            It must be great that can inherit us

            So much as of a thought of ill in him.

Bolingbroke.   Look what I speak, my life shall prove it true:

            That Mowbray hath received eight thousand nobles

            In name of lendings for your Highness' soldiers,

            The which he hath detained for lewd employments,

            Like a false traitor and injurious villain.

Besides, I say, and will in battle prove,

Or here, or elsewhere to the furthest verge

That ever was surveyed by English eye,

That all the treasons for these eighteen years

Complotted and contrivèd in this land

Fetch from false Mowbray, their first head and spring.

Further, I say and further will maintain

Upon his bad life to make all this good,

That he did plot the Duke of Gloucester's death,

Suggest his soon-believing adversaries,

And, consequently, like a traitor coward,

Sluiced out his innocent soul through streams of blood;

Which blood, like sacrificing Abel's, cries

Even from the tongueless caverns of the earth

To me for justice and rough chastisement:

And, by the glorious worth of my descent,

This arm shall do it, or this life be spent.

Richard.	How high a pitch his resolution soars!
	Thomas of Norfolk, what say'st thou to this?
Mowbray.	O! Let my sovereign turn away his face,
	And bid his ears a little while be deaf,
	Till I have told this slander of his blood
	How God and good men hate so foul a liar.
Richard.	Mowbray, impartial are our eyes and ears.
	Were he my brother, nay, my kingdom's heir,
	As he is but my father's brother's son,
	Now by my scepter's awe I make a vow,
	Such neighbor nearness to our sacred blood
	Should nothing privilege him, nor partialize
	The unstooping firmness of my upright soul.
	He is our subject, Mowbray, so art thou:
	Free speech and fearless I to thee allow.

Mowbray.   Then, Bolingbroke, as low as to thy heart,

Through the false passage of thy throat, thou liest.

Three parts of that receipt I had for Calais

Disbursed I duly to his Highness' soldiers;

The other part reserved I by consent,

For that my sovereign liege was in my debt

Upon remainder of a dear account,

Since last I went to France to fetch his Queen.

Now swallow down that lie. For Gloucester's death,

I slew him not; but, to my own disgrace,

Neglected my sworn duty in that case.

For you, my noble Lord of Lancaster,

The honorable father to my foe,

Once did I lay an ambush for your life,

A trespass that doth vex my grievèd soul;

But, ere I last received the sacrament,

I did confess it, and exactly begged

Your grace's pardon, and I hope I had it.

This is my fault: as for the rest appealed,

It issues from the rancor of a villain,

A recreant and most degenerate traitor;

Which in myself I boldly will defend,

And interchangeably hurl down my gage

Upon this overweening traitor's foot,

To prove myself a loyal gentleman

Even in the best blood chambered in his bosom.

In haste whereof, most heartily I pray

Your highness to assign our trial day.

Richard. Wrath-kindled gentlemen, be ruled by me.

Let's purge this choler without letting blood:

This we prescribe, though no physician;

Deep malice makes too deep incision;

Forget, forgive, conclude, and be agreed;

Our doctors say this is no month to bleed.

Good uncle, let this end where it begun:

We'll calm the Duke of Norfolk, you your son.

Gaunt.	To be a make-peace shall become my age:
	Throw down, my son, the Duke of Norfolk's gage.
Richard.	And Norfolk, throw down his.
Gaunt.	When, Harry, when?
	Obedience bids I should not bid again.
Richard.	Norfolk, throw down; we bid—there is no boot.
Mowbray.	Myself I throw, dread sovereign, at thy foot.
	My life thou shalt command, but not my shame:
	The one my duty owes; but my fair name
	Despite of death that lives upon my grave,
	To dark dishonor's use thou shalt not have.
	I am disgraced, impeached, and baffled here,
	Pierced to the soul with slander's venomed spear,
	The which no balm can cure but his heart-blood
	Which breathed this poison.

Richard.   Rage must be withstoood.

          Give me his gage; lions make leopards tame.

Mowbray. Yea, but not change his spots. Take but my shame,

          And I resign my gage. My dear, dear lord,

          The purest treasure mortal times afford

          Is spotless reputation—that away,

          Men are but gilded loam, or painted clay.

          A jewel in a ten-times-barred-up chest

          Is a bold spirit in a loyal breast;

          Mine honor is my life, both grow in one;

          Take honor from me, and my life is done;

          Then, dear my liege, mine honor let me try;

          In that I live, and for that will I die.

Richard. Cousin, throw up your gage; do you begin.

Bolingbroke. O, God defend my soul from such deep sin!
Shall I seem crestfallen in my father's sight?
Or with pale beggar-fear impeach my height
Before this out-dared dastard? Ere my tongue
Shall wound my honor with such feeble wrong,
Or sound so base a parle, my teeth shall tear
The slavish motive of recanting fear,
And spit it bleeding in his high disgrace,
Where shame doth harbor, even in Mowbray's face.
        [*Exit Gaunt*]

Richard. We were not born to sue, but to command:
Which since we cannot do to make you friends,
Be ready, as your lives shall answer it,
At Coventry upon Saint Lambert's day.
There shall your swords and lances arbitrate

The swelling difference of your settled hate:
Since we cannot atone you, we shall see
Justice design the victor's chivalry.
Lord Marshal, command our officers-at-arms
Be ready to direct these home alarms.

[Exit Richard with others]

SCENE II
LONDON. GAUNT'S HOUSE

[Enter John of Gaunt with the Duchess of Gloucester]

Gaunt.   Alas, the part I had in Woodstock's blood

Doth more solicit me than your exclaims

To stir against the butchers of his life;

But since correction lieth in those hands

Which made the fault that we cannot correct,

Put we our quarrel to the will of heaven,

Who, when they see the hours ripe on earth,

Will rain hot vengeance on offenders' heads.

Duchess.   Finds brotherhood in thee no sharper spur?

Hath love in thy old blood no living fire?

Edward's seven sons, whereof thyself art one,

Were as seven vials of his sacred blood,

Or seven fair branches springing from one root.

Some of those seven are dried by nature's course,

Some of those branches by the destinies cut:

But Thomas, my dear lord, my life, my Gloucester,

One vial full of Edward's sacred blood,

One flourishing branch of his most royal root,

Is cracked, and all the precious liquor spilt,

Is hacked down, and his summer leaves all faded

By Envy's hand and Murder's bloody ax.

Ah! Gaunt, his blood was thine; that bed, that womb,

That metal, that self mold that fashioned thee,

Made him a man: and though thou livest and breathest,

Yet art thou slain in him; thou dost consent

In some large measure to thy father's death,

In that thou seest thy wretched brother die,

Who was the model of thy father's life.

Call it not patience, Gaunt, it is despair:

In suff'ring thus thy brother to be slaught'red,

Thou showest the naked pathway to thy life,

Teaching stern Murder how to butcher thee.

That which in mean men we entitle patience

Is pale cold cowardice in noble breasts.

What shall I say? To safeguard thine own life,

The best way is to venge my Gloucester's death.

Gaunt. God's is the quarrel; for God's substitute,

His deputy anointed in His sight,

Hath caused his death, the which if wrongfully,

Let heaven revenge, for I may never lift

An angry arm against His minister.

Duchess. Where, then, alas, may I complain myself?

Gaunt. To God, the widow's champion and defense.

Duchess. Why, then, I will. Farewell, old Gaunt,

Thou goest to Coventry, there to behold

Our cousin Hereford and fell Mowbray fight.

O! Sit my husband's wrongs on Hereford's spear,

That it may enter butcher Mowbray's breast;

Or if misfortune miss the first career,

Be Mowbray's sins so heavy in his bosom,

That they may break his foaming courser's back,

And throw the rider headlong in the lists,

A caitiff recreant to my cousin Hereford.

Farewell, old Gaunt; thy sometimes brother's wife

With her companion, Grief, must end her life.

Gaunt. Sister, farewell, I must to Coventry:

As much good stay with thee, as go with me.

Duchess.   Yet one word more: grief boundeth where it falls,

Not with the empty hollowness, but weight.

I take my leave before I have begun,

For sorrow ends not when it seemeth done.

Commend me to thy brother, Edmund York.

Lo! This is all: nay, yet depart not so;

Though this be all, do not so quickly go.

I shall remember more. Bid him . . . Ah! What?

With all good speed at Plashy visit me.

Alack! And what shall good old York there see

But empty lodgings and unfurnished walls,

Unpeopled offices, untrodden stones,

And what hear there for welcome but my groans?

Therefore commend me, let him not come there,

To seek out sorrow that dwells everywhere.

Desolate, desolate will I hence and die!

The last leave of thee takes my weeping eye.

[*Exeunt*]

[Enter Lord Marshal and the Duke Aumerle]

Marshal. My Lord Aumerle, is Harry Hereford armed?

Aumerle. Yea, at all points, and longs to enter in.

Marshal. The Duke of Norfolk, sprightfully and bold,
Stays but the summons of the appellant's trumpet.

Aumerle. Why, then, the champions are prepared, and stay
For nothing but his Majesty's approach.

> *[The trumpets sound. The King enters with his
> nobles; including Gaunt, Bushy, Bagot, Green.
> When they are set, enter Mowbray, the Duke
> of Norfolk, in arms, defendant, and a Herald]*

Richard. Marshal, demand of yonder champion
The cause of his arrival here in arms;
Ask him his name; and orderly proceed
To swear him in the justice of his cause.

Marshal. In God's name and the King's, say who thou art
And why thou comest thus knightly clad in arms,
Against what man thou com'st, and what thy quarrel.
Speak truly on thy knighthood and thy oath,
As so defend thee heaven and thy valor.

Mowbray. My name is Thomas Mowbray, Duke of Norfolk,
Who hither come engagèd by my oath—
Which God defend a knight should violate!
Both to defend my loyalty and truth
To God, my king, and my succeeding issue,
Against the Duke of Hereford that appeals me;
And by the grace of God, and this mine arm,
To prove him in defending of myself
A traitor to my God, my king, and me;
And as I truly fight, defend me, heaven!

> [*The trumpets sound. Enter Bolingbroke,
> Duke of Hereford, appellant, in armor*]

Richard. Marshal, demand of yonder knight in arms,
Both who he is, and why he cometh hither
Thus plated in habiliments of war,
And formally, according to our law,
Depose him in the justice of his cause.

Marshal. What is thy name? And wherefore com'st thou hither
Before King Richard in his royal lists?
Against whom comest thou? And what's thy quarrel?
Speak like a true knight, so defend thee heaven.

Bolingbroke. Harry of Hereford, Lancaster and Derby
Am I, who ready here do stand in arms
To prove by God's grace, and my body's valor
In lists, on Thomas Mowbray, Duke of Norfolk,
That he is a traitor, foul and dangerous,
To God of heaven, King Richard and to me:
And as I truly fight, defend me, heaven!

Marshal.	On pain of death, no person be so bold
	Or daring-hardy as to touch the lists,
	Except the Marshal and such officers
	Appointed to direct these fair designs.
Bolingbroke.	Lord Marshal, let me kiss my Sovereign's hand,
	And bow my knee before his Majesty;
	For Mowbray and myself are like two men
	That vow a long and weary pilgrimage:
	Then let us take a ceremonious leave
	And loving farewell of our several friends.
Marshal.	The appellant in all duty greets your Highness,
	And craves to kiss your hand and take his leave.
Richard.	We will descend and fold him in our arms.
	Cousin of Hereford, as thy cause is right,
	So be thy fortune in this royal fight:
	Farewell, my blood, which if today thou shed,
	Lament we may, but not revenge thee dead.

Bolingbroke. O, let no noble eye profane a tear
For me, if I be gored with Mowbray's spear:
As confident as is the falcon's flight
Against a bird, do I with Mowbray fight.
My loving lord, I take my leave of you;
Of you, my noble cousin, Lord Aumerle,
Not sick, although I have to do with death,
But lusty, young, and cheerly drawing breath.
Lo! As at English feasts, so I regreet
The daintiest last, to make the end most sweet.
O thou, the earthly author of my blood,
Whose youthful spirit in me regenerate
Doth with a twofold vigor lift me up
To reach at victory above my head,
Add proof unto mine armor with thy prayers,
And with thy blessings steel my lance's point,
That it may enter Mowbray's waxen coat
And furbish new the name of John a Gaunt
Even in the lusty havior of his son.

Gaunt. God in thy good cause make thee prosperous;

Be swift like lightning in the execution,

And let thy blows doubly redoubled

Fall like amazing thunder on the casque

Of thy adverse pernicious enemy:

Rouse up thy youthful blood, be valiant and live.

Bolingbroke. Mine innocency and St. George to thrive!

Mowbray. However God or fortune cast my lot,

There lives or dies, true to King Richard's throne,

A loyal, just and upright gentleman.

Never did captive with a freer heart

Cast off his chains of bondage, and embrace

His golden, uncontrolled enfranchisement

More than my dancing soul doth celebrate

This feast of battle with mine adversary.

Most mighty liege, and my companion peers,

Take from my mouth the wish of happy years;

As gentle and as jocund as to jest

Go I to fight: truth hath a quiet breast.

Richard.	Farewell, my lord; securely I espy
	Virtue with valor couchèd in thine eye.
	Order the trial, Marshal, and begin.
Marshal.	Harry of Hereford, Lancaster and Derby,
	Receive thy lance, and God defend the right.
Bolingbroke.	Strong as a tower in hope, I cry Amen.
Marshal.	Go bear this lance to Thomas, Duke of Norfolk.
First Herald.	Harry of Hereford, Lancaster and Derby,
	Stands here for God, his Sovereign and himself,
	On pain to be found false and recreant,
	To prove the Duke of Norfolk, Thomas Mowbray,
	A traitor to his God, his king, and him,
	And dares him to set forward to the fight.
Second Herald.	Here standeth Thomas Mowbray, Duke of Norfolk,
	On pain to be found false and recreant,
	Both to defend himself, and to approve
	Henry of Hereford, Lancaster and Derby,
	To God, his sovereign, and to him disloyal,
	Courageously and with a free desire
	Attending but the signal to begin.

Marshal. Sound trumpets; and set forward combatants!

        [*A charge sounded*]

    Stay, the King hath thrown his warder down.

Richard. Let them lay by their helmets and their spears

    And both return back to their chairs again.

    Withdraw with us, and let the trumpets sound,

    While we return these dukes what we decree.

        [*A long flourish*]

    Draw near,

    And list what with our council we have done.

    For that our kingdom's earth should not be soiled

    With that dear blood which it hath fosterèd;

    And for our eyes do hate the dire aspect

    Of civil wounds plowed up with neighbor's sword,

    And for we think the eagle-wingèd pride

    Of sky-aspiring and ambitious thoughts

    With rival-hating envy set on you

    To wake our peace, which in our country's cradle

    Draws the sweet infant breath of gentle sleep,

    Which so roused up with boist'rous untuned drums,

With harsh resounding trumpets' dreadful bray,

And grating shock of wrathful iron arms,

Might from our quiet confines fright fair Peace,

And make us wade even in our kindred's blood;

Therefore we banish you our territories:

You, cousin Hereford, upon pain of life,

Till twice five summers have enriched our fields,

Shall not regreet our fair dominions,

But tread the stranger paths of banishment.

Bolingbroke. Your will be done: this must my comfort be,

That sun that warms you here shall shine on me,

And those his golden beams to you here lent

Shall point on me, and gild my banishment.

Richard. Norfolk, for thee remains a heavier doom

Which I with some unwillingness pronounce:

The sly slow hours shall not determinate

The dateless limit of thy dear exile;

The hopeless word, of Never to return,

Breathe I against thee, upon pain of life.

Mowbray. A heavy sentence, my most sovereign liege,
And all unlooked for from your Highness' mouth:
A dearer merit, not so deep a maim
As to be cast forth in the common air
Have I deservèd at your Highness' hands!
The language I have learnt these forty years,
My native English, now I must forgo,
And now my tongue's use is to me no more
Than an unstringèd viol or a harp,
Or like a cunning instrument cased up,
Or being open, put into his hands
That knows no touch to tune the harmony.
Within my mouth you have enjailed my tongue,
Doubly portcullised with my teeth and lips,
And dull unfeeling barren ignorance
Is made my jailer to attend on me.
I am too old to fawn upon a nurse,
Too far in years to be a pupil now;
What is thy sentence then but speechless death,
Which robs my tongue from breathing native breath?

Richard.   It boots thee not to be compassionate:

After our sentence, plaining comes too late.

Mowbray.   Then thus I turn me from my country's light,

To dwell in solemn shades of endless night.

[*Turns to go*]

Richard.   Return again, and take an oath with thee.

Lay on our royal sword your banished hands;

Swear by the duty that you owe to God—

Our part therein we banish with yourselves—

To keep the oath that we administer:

You never shall—so help you truth and God!—

Embrace each other's love in banishment,

Nor never look upon each other's face,

Nor never write, regreet, nor reconcile

This louring tempest of your home-bred hate,

Nor never by advisèd purpose meet

To plot, contrive, or complot any ill

'Gainst us, our state, our subjects, or our land.

Bolingbroke. I swear.

Mowbray.   And I, to keep all this.

Bolingbroke. Norfolk, so far as to mine enemy—
By this time, had the King permitted us,
One of our souls had wandered in the air,
Banished this frail sepulcher of our flesh,
As now our flesh is banished from this land:
Confess thy treasons ere thou fly the realm;
Since thou hast far to go, bear not along
The clogging burden of a guilty soul.

Mowbray. No, Bolingbroke, if ever I were traitor,
My name be blotted from the book of life,
And I from heaven banished as from hence!
But what thou art, God, thou, and I, do know,
And all too soon, I fear, the King shall rue.
Farewell my liege, now no way can I stray:
Save back to England all the world's my way.
            [*Exit*]

Richard. Uncle, even in the glasses of thine eyes

I see thy grievèd heart: thy sad aspect

Hath from the number of his banished years

Plucked four away. [*To Bolingbroke*] Six frozen winters spent,

Return with welcome home from banishment.

Bolingbroke. How long a time lies in one little word.

Four lagging winters and four wanton springs

End in a word—such is the breath of kings.

Gaunt. I thank my liege that in regard of me

He shortens four years of my son's exile,

But little vantage shall I reap thereby:

For ere the six years that he hath to spend

Can change their moons and bring their times about,

My oil-dried lamp and time-bewasted light

Shall be extinct with age and endless night;

My inch of taper will be burnt and done,

And blindfold Death not let me see my son.

Richard. Why! Uncle, thou hast many years to live.

Gaunt.   But not a minute, King, that thou canst give;

Shorten my days thou canst with sullen sorrow

And pluck nights from me, but not lend a morrow;

Thou canst help time to furrow me with age,

But stop no wrinkle in his pilgrimage:

Thy word is current with him for my death,

But dead, thy kingdom cannot buy my breath.

Richard.   Thy son is banished upon good advice,

Whereto thy tongue a party-verdict gave:

Why at our justice seem'st thou then to lour?

Gaunt.   Things sweet to taste prove in digestion sour.

You urged me as a judge, but I had rather

You would have bid me argue like a father.

O, had it been a stranger, not my child,

To smooth his fault I should have been more mild:

A partial slander sought I to avoid,

And in the sentence my own life destroyed.

Alas! I looked when some of you should say

I was too strict to make mine own away;

But you gave leave to my unwilling tongue

Against my will to do myself this wrong.

Richard. Cousin, farewell, and uncle, bid him so;

Six years we banish him, and he shall go.

[Flourish. Exit King Richard with his train]

Aumerle. Cousin, farewell; what presence must not know,

From where you do remain let paper show.

Marshal. My lord, no leave take I, for I will ride

As far as land will let me by your side.

Gaunt. O, to what purpose dost thou hoard thy words,

That thou returnest no greeting to thy friends?

Bolingbroke. I have too few to take my leave of you,

When the tongue's office should be prodigal

To breathe the abundant dolor of the heart.

Gaunt. Thy grief is but thy absence for a time.

Bolingbroke.	Joy absent, grief is present for that time.
Gaunt.	What is six winters? They are quickly gone.
Bolingbroke.	To men in joy; but grief makes one hour ten.
Gaunt.	Call it a travel that thou tak'st for pleasure.
Bolingbroke.	My heart will sigh when I miscall it so,
	Which finds it an enforcèd pilgrimage.
Gaunt.	The sullen passage of thy weary steps
	Esteem as foil wherein thou art to set
	The precious jewel of thy home return.
Bolingbroke.	Nay, rather, every tedious stride I make
	Will but remember me what a deal of world
	I wander from the jewels that I love.
	Must I not serve a long apprenticehood
	To foreign passages, and in the end,
	Having my freedom, boast of nothing else
	But that I was a journeyman to grief?

Gaunt. All places that the eye of heaven visits

Are to a wise man ports and happy havens.

Teach thy necessity to reason thus:

There is no virtue like necessity.

Think not the King did banish thee,

But thou the King. Woe doth the heavier sit

Where it perceives it is but faintly borne.

Go, say I sent thee forth to purchase honor,

And not the King exiled thee; or suppose

Devouring pestilence hangs in our air,

And thou art flying to a fresher clime.

Look what thy soul holds dear, imagine it

To lie that way thou goest, not whence thou com'st.

Suppose the singing birds musicians,

The grass whereon thou tread'st the presence strewed,

The flowers fair ladies, and thy steps no more

Than a delightful measure or a dance;

For gnarling sorrow hath less power to bite

The man that mocks at it and sets it light.

Bolingbroke. O, who can hold a fire in his hand

By thinking on the frosty Caucasus?

Or cloy the hungry edge of appetite

By bare imagination of a feast?

Or wallow naked in December snow

By thinking on fantastic summer's heat?

O, no! The apprehension of the good

Gives but the greater feeling to the worse.

Fell Sorrow's tooth doth never rankle more

Than when he bites, but lanceth not the sore.

Gaunt. Come, come, my son, I'll bring thee on thy way.

Had I thy youth and cause, I would not stay.

Bolingbroke. Then England's ground, farewell; sweet soil, adieu;

My mother and my nurse that bears me yet!

Where'er I wander, boast of this I can:

Though banished, yet a true-born Englishman.

   [Exeunt]

*[Enter the King, with Bagot, Green, etc. at
one door, and the Lord Aumerle at another]*

Richard.   We did observe. Cousin Aumerle,

How far brought you high Hereford on his way?

Aumerle.   I brought high Hereford, if you call him so,

But to the next high way, and there I left him.

Richard.   And say, what store of parting tears were shed?

Aumerle.   Faith, none for me, except the northeast wind,

Which then blew bitterly against our faces,

Awaked the sleeping rheum, and so by chance

Did grace our hollow parting with a tear.

Richard.   What said our cousin when you parted with him?

Aumerle. "Farewell."

And for my heart disdainèd that my tongue

Should so profane the word, that taught me craft

To counterfeit oppression of such grief

That words seemed buried in my sorrow's grave.

Marry, would the word "Farewell" have length'ned hours

And added years to his short banishment,

He should have had a volume of farewells;

But since it would not, he had none of me.

Richard. He is our cousin, cousin, but 'tis doubt,

When time shall call him home from banishment,

Whether our kinsman come to see his friends.

Ourself and Bushy, Bagot here and Green,

Observed his courtship to the common people,

How he did seem to dive into their hearts

With humble and familiar courtesy,

What reverence he did throw away on slaves,

Wooing poor craftsmen with the craft of smiles

And patient underbearing of his fortune,

As 'twere to banish their affects with him.

Off goes his bonnet to an oyster-wench;

A brace of draymen bid God speed him well,

And had the tribute of his supple knee,

With "Thanks, my countrymen, my loving friends";

As were our England in reversion his,

And he our subjects' next degree in hope.

Green. Well, he is gone, and with him go these thoughts.
Now for the rebels which stand out in Ireland;
Expedient manage must be made, my liege,
Ere further leisure yield them further means
For their advantage and your Highness' loss.

Richard. We will ourself in person to this war,
And for our coffers with too great a court
And liberal largess are grown somewhat light,
We are enforced to farm our royal realm,
The revenue whereof shall furnish us
For our affairs in hand. If that come short,
Our substitutes at home shall have blank charters;
Whereto, when they shall know what men are rich,
They shall subscribe them for large sums of gold,
And send them after to supply our wants,
For we will make for Ireland presently.
   [*Enter Bushy*]
Bushy, what news?

Bushy.   Old John of Gaunt is grievous sick, my Lord,

Suddenly taken, and hath sent posthaste

To intreat your Majesty to visit him.

Richard.   Where lies he?

Bushy.   At Ely House.

Richard.   Now put it, God, in the physician's mind

To help him to his grave immediately!

The lining of his coffers shall make coats

To deck our soldiers for these Irish wars.

Come, gentlemen, let's all go visit him;

Pray God we may make haste and come too late!

All.   Amen!

[Exeunt]

ACT TWO

SCENE I
LONDON. ELY HOUSE

[Enter John of Gaunt, sick, with the Duke of York
and the Earl of Northumberland, Attendants, etc.]

Gaunt. Will the King come, that I may breathe my last
In wholesome counsel to his unstaid youth?

York. Vex not yourself, nor strive not with your breath,
For all in vain comes counsel to his ear.

Gaunt. O, but they say the tongues of dying men
Enforce attention like deep harmony:
Where words are scarce they are seldom spent in vain,
For they breathe truth that breathe their words in pain;
He that no more must say is listened more
Than they whom youth and ease have taught to glose;
More are men's ends marked than their lives before;
The setting sun, and music at the close,
As the last taste of sweets is sweetest last,
Writ in remembrance more than things long past:
Though Richard my life's counsel would not hear,
My death's sad tale may yet undeaf his ear.

York. No, it is stopped with other flattering sounds:
As praises—of whose taste the wise are fond—
Lascivious meters, to whose venom sound
The open ear of youth doth always listen;
Report of fashions in proud Italy
Whose manners still our tardy-apish nation
Limps after in base imitation.
Where doth the world thrust forth a vanity—
So it be new, there's no respect how vile—
That is not quickly buzzed into his ears?
Then all too late comes counsel to be heard,
Where will doth mutiny with wit's regard.
Direct not him whose way himself will choose:
'Tis breath thou lack'st, and that breath wilt thou lose.

Gaunt.   Methinks I am a prophet new inspired,

And thus expiring do foretell of him:

His rash fierce blaze of riot cannot last,

For violent fires soon burn out themselves.

Small showers last long, but sudden storms are short;

He tires betimes that spurs too fast betimes;

With eager feeding, food doth choke the feeder.

Light vanity, insatiate cormorant,

Consuming means, soon preys upon itself.

This royal throne of kings, this scept'red isle,

This earth of majesty, this seat of Mars,

This other Eden, demi-paradise,

This fortress built by Nature for herself

Against infection and the hand of war,

This happy breed of men, this little world,

This precious stone set in the silver sea

Which serves it in the office of a wall,

Or as a moat defensive to a house,

Against the envy of less happier lands,

This blessed plot, this earth, this realm, this England,

This nurse, this teeming womb of royal kings,

Feared by their breed, and famous by their birth,

Renownèd for their deeds as far from home,

For Christian service and true chivalry,

As is the sepulcher in stubborn Jewry

Of the world's ransom, blessèd Mary's son,

This land of such dear souls, this dear dear land—

Dear for her reputation through the world—

Is now leased out—I die pronouncing it—

Like to a tenement or pelting farm.

England, bound in with the triumphant sea,

Whose rocky shore beats back the envious siege

Of wat'ry Neptune, is now bound in with shame,

With inky blots, and rotten parchment bonds.

That England that was wont to conquer others

Hath made a shameful conquest of itself.

Ah! Would the scandal vanish with my life,

How happy then were my ensuing death!

[Enter King and Queen, etc. Ross, Bushy,
Green, Bagot, Aumerle, and Willoughby]

York. The King is come; deal mildly with his youth,

For young hot colts being raged do rage the more.

Queen. How fares our noble uncle, Lancaster?

Richard. What comfort, man? How is't with aged Gaunt?

Gaunt. O, how that name befits my composition!

Old Gaunt indeed, and gaunt in being old!

Within me Grief hath kept a tedious fast;

And who abstains from meat that is not gaunt?

For sleeping England long time have I watched:

Watching breeds leanness, leanness is all gaunt.

The pleasure that some fathers feed upon

Is my strict fast—I mean my children's looks—

And therein fasting hast thou made me gaunt;

Gaunt am I for the grave, gaunt as a grave

Whose hollow womb inherits naught but bones.

Richard.	Can sick men play so nicely with their names?
Gaunt.	No, misery makes sport to mock itself:
	Since thou dost seek to kill my name in me,
	I mock my name, great King, to flatter thee.
Richard.	Should dying men flatter with those that live?
Gaunt.	No, no, men living flatter those that die.
Richard.	Thou, now a-dying, sayest thou flatterest me.
Gaunt.	O no, thou diest, though I the sicker be.
Richard.	I am in health, I breathe, and see thee ill.
Gaunt.	Now he that made me knows I see thee ill;
	Ill in myself to see, and in thee seeing ill.
	Thy deathbed is no lesser than thy land,
	Wherein thou liest in reputation sick;
	And thou, too careless patient as thou art,
	Commit'st thy anointed body to the cure

Of those physicians that first wounded thee.
A thousand flatterers sit within thy crown,
Whose compass is no bigger than thy head,
And yet incagèd in so small a verge
The waste is no whit lesser than thy land.
O, had thy grandsire with a prophet's eye
Seen how his son's son should destroy his sons,
From forth thy reach he would have laid thy shame,
Deposing thee before thou wert possessed,
Which art possessed now to depose thyself.
Why, cousin, wert thou regent of the world,
It were a shame to let this land by lease;
But for thy world enjoying but this land
Is it not more than shame to shame it so?
Landlord of England art thou now, not king;
Thy state of law is bondslave to the law,
And thou—

Richard.   [*Interrupting*] A lunatic, lean-witted fool,

Presuming on an ague's privilege,

Darest with thy frozen admonition

Make pale our cheek, chasing the royal blood

With fury from his native residence.

Now, by my seat's right-royal majesty

Wert thou not brother to great Edward's son,

This tongue that runs so roundly in thy head

Should run thy head from thy unreverent shoulders.

Gaunt.   O, spare me not, my brother Edward's son,

For that I was his father Edward's son,

That blood already like the pelican

Hast thou tapped out and drunkenly caroused:

My brother Gloucester, plain well-meaning soul—

Whom fair befall in heaven 'mongst happy souls!—

May be a precedent and witness good

That thou respect'st not spilling Edward's blood.

Join with the present sickness that I have,

And thy unkindness be like crooked age

To crop at once a too-long-withered flower.

Live in thy shame, but die not shame with thee;

These words hereafter thy tormentors be.

Convey me to my bed, then to my grave;

Love they to live that love and honor have.

[Exit Gaunt, borne by Attendants, and Northumberland]

Richard. And let them die that age and sullens have,

For both hast thou, and both become the grave.

York. I do beseech your Majesty, impute his words

To wayward sickliness and age in him:

He loves you, on my life, and holds you dear

As Harry, Duke of Hereford, were he here.

Richard. Right, you say true, as Herefords' love, so his,

As theirs, so mine; and all be as it is.

[Enter Northumberland]

Northumberland. My liege, old Gaunt commends him to your Majesty.

Richard. What says he?

Northumberland. Nay, nothing, all is said;

His tongue is now a stringless instrument;

Words, life and all, old Lancaster hath spent.

York.   Be York the next that must be bankrout so!

            Though death be poor, it ends a mortal woe.

Richard.   The ripest fruit first falls, and so doth he;

            His time is spent, our pilgrimage must be;

            So much for that. Now for our Irish wars.

            We must supplant those rough rug-headed kernes

            Which live like venom, where no venom else,

            But only they, have privilege to live.

            And for these great affairs do ask some charge,

            Towards our assistance we do seize to us

            The plate, coin, revenues, and movables

            Whereof our uncle Gaunt did stand possessed.

York.   How long shall I be patient? Ah, how long

            Shall tender duty make me suffer wrong?

            Not Gloucester's death, nor Hereford's banishment,

            Nor Gaunt's rebukes, nor England's private wrongs,

            Nor the prevention of poor Bolingbroke

About his marriage, nor my own disgrace,

Have ever made me sour my patient cheek,

Or bend one wrinkle on my Sovereign's face.

I am the last of noble Edward's sons,

Of whom thy father, Prince of Wales, was first:

In war was never lion raged more fierce,

In peace was never gentle lamb more mild,

Than was that young and princely gentleman.

His face thou hast, for even so looked he,

Accomplished with the number of thy hours;

But when he frowned it was against the French,

And not against his friends; his noble hand

Did win what he did spend, and spend not that

Which his triumphant father's hand had won;

His hands were guilty of no kindred blood,

But bloody with the enemies of his kin.

O, Richard, York is too far gone with grief,

Or else he never would compare between—

Richard. Why, uncle, what's the matter?

York.   O my liege,

Pardon me, if you please; if not, I pleased

Not to be pardoned, am content withal.

Seek you to seize and gripe into your hands

The royalties and rights of banished Hereford?

Is not Gaunt dead? And doth not Hereford live?

Was not Gaunt just? And is not Harry true?

Did not the one deserve to have an heir?

Is not his heir a well-deserving son?

Take Hereford's rights away, and take from time

His charters and his customary rights,

Let not tomorrow then ensue today;

Be not thyself. For how art thou a king

But by fair sequence and succession?

Now afore God—God forbid I say true—

If you do wrongfully seize Hereford's rights,

Call in the letters patents that he hath

By his attorneys-general to sue

His livery, and deny his off'red homage,

You pluck a thousand dangers on your head,

You lose a thousand well-disposèd hearts,

And prick my tender patience to those thoughts

Which honor and allegiance cannot think.

Richard. Think what you will, we seize into our hands

His plate, his goods, his money, and his lands.

York. I'll not be by the while. My liege, farewell.

What will ensue hereof there's none can tell:

But by bad courses may be understood

That their events can never fall out good.

[*Exit*]

Richard. Go, Bushy, to the Earl of Wiltshire straight;

Bid him repair to us to Ely House,

To see this business. Tomorrow next

We will for Ireland—and 'tis time, I trow;

And we create in absence of ourself

Our uncle York Lord Governor of England,

For he is just, and always loved us well.

Come on, our queen, tomorrow must we part;

Be merry, for our time of stay is short.

[*Flourish. Exeunt the King and Queen. Manent
Northumberland, with Willoughby, and Ross*]

Northumberland.   Well, lords, the Duke of Lancaster is dead.

Ross.   And living too, for now his son is duke.

Willoughby.   Barely in title, not in revenues.

Northumberland.   Richly in both, if justice had her right.

Ross.   My heart is great, but it must break with silence
Ere't be disburdened with a liberal tongue.

Northumberland.   Nay, speak thy mind, and let him ne'er speak more
That speaks thy words again to do thee harm.

Willoughby.   Tends that that thou would'st speak to the Duke of Hereford?
If it be so, out with it boldly, man;
Quick is mine ear to hear of good towards him.

Ross.   No good at all that I can do for him,
Unless you call it good to pity him,
Bereft, and gelded of his patrimony.

Northumberland.   Now, afore God, 'tis shame such wrongs are borne

In him a royal prince and many moe

Of noble blood in this declining land!

The King is not himself, but basely led

By flatterers; and what they will inform

Merely in hate 'gainst any of us all,

That will the King severely prosecute

'Gainst us, our lives, our children, and our heirs.

Ross.   The commons hath he pilled with grievous taxes

And quite lost their hearts. The nobles hath he fined

For ancient quarrels and quite lost their hearts.

Willoughby.   And daily new exactions are devised,

As blanks, benevolences, and I wot not what:

But what, a God's name, doth become of this?

Northumberland.   Wars hath not wasted it, for warred he hath not,

But basely yielded upon compromise

That which his noble ancestors achieved with blows:

More hath he spent in peace than they in wars.

Ross.	The Earl of Wiltshire hath the realm in farm.
Willoughby.	The King's grown bankrout like a broken man.
Northumberland.	Reproach and dissolution hangeth over him.
Ross.	He hath not money for these Irish wars,
	His burdenous taxations notwithstanding,
	But by the robbing of the banished Duke.
Northumberland.	His noble kinsman—most degenerate king!
	But, lords, we hear this fearful tempest sing,
	Yet seek no shelter to avoid the storm:
	We see the wind sit sore upon our sails,
	And yet we strike not, but securely perish.
Ross.	We see the very wrack that we must suffer,
	And unavoided is the danger now,
	For suffering so the causes of our wrack.
Northumberland.	Not so; even through the hollow eyes of death
	I spy life peering, but I dare not say
	How near the tidings of our comfort is.
Willoughby.	Nay, let us share thy thoughts, as thou dost ours.

Ross. Be confident to speak, Northumberland;

We three are but thyself, and speaking so

Thy words are but as thoughts: therefore be bold.

Northumberland. Then thus: I have from le Port Blanc, a bay

In Brittaine, received intelligence

That Harry, Duke of Hereford, Rainold, Lord Cobham,

[The son of Richard, Earl of Arundel,]

That late broke from the Duke of Exeter,

His brother, Archbishop, late of Canterbury,

Sir Thomas Erpingham, Sir Thomas Ramston,

Sir John Norbery, Sir Robert Waterton, and Francis Quoint—

All these well furnished by the Duke of Brittaine

With eight tall ships, three thousand men of war,

Are making hither with all due expedience,

And shortly mean to touch our northern shore.

Perhaps they had ere this, but that they stay

The first departing of the King for Ireland.

If then we shall shake off our slavish yoke,

Imp out our drooping country's broken wing,

Redeem from broking pawn the blemished crown,

Wipe off the dust that hides our scepter's gilt,

And make high majesty look like itself,

Away with me in post to Ravenspurgh;

But if you faint, as fearing to do so,

Stay, and be secret, and myself will go.

Ross. To horse, to horse, urge doubts to them that fear.

Willoughby. Hold out my horse, and I will first be there.

[*Exeunt*]

SCENE II
WINDSOR CASTLE

[Enter the Queen, Bushy, Bagot]

Bushy.   Madam, your Majesty is too much sad.

You promised, when you parted with the King,

To lay aside life-harming heaviness,

And entertain a cheerful disposition.

Queen.   To please the King I did: to please myself

I cannot do it; yet I know no cause

Why I should welcome such a guest as Grief,

Save bidding farewell to so sweet a guest

As my sweet Richard. Yet again methinks

Some unborn sorrow ripe in Fortune's womb

Is coming towards me; and my inward soul

With nothing trembles—at something it grieves

More than with parting from my lord the King.

Bushy. Each substance of a grief hath twenty shadows,

Which shows like grief itself, but is not so;

For Sorrow's eye, glazèd with blinding tears,

Divides one thing entire to many objects,

Like perspectives which, rightly gazed upon,

Show nothing but confusion; eyed awry,

Distinguish form. So your sweet Majesty,

Looking awry upon your lord's departure,

Find shapes of grief more than himself to wail,

Which looked on as it is, is nought but shadows

Of what it is not; then, thrice-gracious Queen,

More than your lord's departure weep not: more's not seen,

Or if it be, 'tis with false Sorrow's eye,

Which for things true weeps things imaginary.

Queen. It may be so; but yet my inward soul

Persuades me it is otherwise. Howe'er it be,

I cannot but be sad—so heavy sad,

As, though on thinking on no thought I think,

Makes me with heavy nothing faint and shrink.

Bushy. 'Tis nothing but conceit, my gracious lady.

Queen. 'Tis nothing less: conceit is still derived

    From some forefather grief; mine is not so,

    For nothing hath begot my something grief,

    Or something hath the nothing that I grieve:

    'Tis in reversion that I do possess,

    But what it is that is not yet known what,

    I cannot name; 'tis nameless woe I wot.

        [Enter Green]

Green. God save your Majesty! And well met, gentlemen.

    I hope the King is not yet shipped for Ireland.

Queen. Why hopest thou so? 'Tis better hope he is,

    For his designs crave haste, his haste good hope:

    Then wherefore dost thou hope he is not shipped?

Green. That he our hope might have retired his power

    And driven into despair an enemy's hope,

    Who strongly hath set footing in this land:

    The banished Bolingbroke repeals himself,

    And with uplifted arms is safe arrived

    At Ravenspurgh.

Queen.	Now God in heaven forbid!
Green.	Ah, madam! 'Tis too true; and that is worse,
	The Lord Northumberland, his son, young Henry Percy,
	The lords of Ross, Beaumond, and Willoughby,
	With all their powerful friends are fled to him.
Bushy.	Why have you not proclaimed Northumberland
	And all the rest revolted faction, traitors?
Green.	We have: whereupon the Earl of Worcester
	Hath broken his staff, resigned his stewardship,
	And all the household servants fled with him
	To Bolingbroke.
Queen.	So, Green, thou art the midwife to my woe,
	And Bolingbroke, my sorrow's dismal heir;
	Now hath my soul brought forth her prodigy,
	And I, a gasping, new-delivered mother,
	Have woe to woe, sorrow to sorrow, joined.
Bushy.	Despair not, madam.

Queen.   Who shall hinder me?

I will despair and be at enmity

With cozening Hope: he is a flatterer,

A parasite, a keeper-back of Death,

Who gently would dissolve the bands of life

Which false Hope lingers in extremity.

[Enter the Duke of York]

Green.   Here comes the Duke of York.

Queen.   With signs of war about his aged neck.

O, full of careful business are his looks!

Uncle, for God's sake, speak comfortable words.

York.   Should I do so, I should belie my thoughts.

Comfort's in heaven, and we are on the earth,

Where nothing lives but crosses, cares, and grief.

Your husband, he is gone to save far off,

Whilst others come to make him lose at home.

Here am I left to underprop his land,

Who, weak with age, cannot support myself.

Now comes the sick hour that his surfeit made;

Now shall he try his friends that flattered him.

[Enter Servingman]

Servingman.	My lord, your son was gone before I came.
York.	He was? Why so, go all which way it will.
	The nobles, they are fled, the commons cold,
	And will, I fear, revolt on Hereford's side.
	Sirrah, get thee to Plashy to my sister Gloucester;
	Bid her send me presently a thousand pound.
	Hold, take my ring.
Servingman.	My lord, I had forgot to tell your lordship:
	Today as I came by I callèd there—
	But I shall grieve you to report the rest.
York.	What is't, knave?
Servingman.	An hour before I came the Duchess died.
York.	God for his mercy, what a tide of woes
	Comes rushing on this woeful land at once.
	I know not what to do. I would to God—
	So my untruth had not provoked him to it—
	The King had cut off my head with my brother's.
	What! Are there no posts despatched for Ireland?
	How shall we do for money for these wars?
	Come, sister—cousin, I would say—pray pardon me.

Go fellow, get thee home, provide some carts,

And bring away the armor that is there.

    [Exit Servingman]

Gentlemen, will you go muster men?

If I know how or which way to order these affairs,

Thus disorderly thrust into my hands,

Never believe me. Both are my kinsmen.

Th' one is my sovereign, whom both my oath

And duty bids defend; t'other again

Is my kinsman, whom the King hath wronged,

Whom conscience and my kindred bids to right.

Well, somewhat we must do. Come, cousin,

I'll dispose of you. Gentlemen, go muster up your men,

And meet me presently at Berkeley.

I should to Plashy too,

But time will not permit. All is uneven,

And everything is left at six and seven.

    [Exeunt Duke, Queen. Manent Bushy, Bagot, Green]

Bushy.   The wind sits fair for news to go for Ireland,
But none returns. For us to levy power
Proportionable to the enemy
Is all unpossible.

Green.   Besides, our nearness to the King in love
Is near the hate of those love not the King.

Bagot.   And that is the wavering commons, for their love
Lies in their purses, and whoso empties them
By so much fills their hearts with deadly hate.

Bushy.   Wherein the King stands generally condemned.

Bagot.   If judgment lie in them, then so do we,
Because we ever have been near the King.

Green.   Well, I will for refuge straight to Bristow Castle.
The Earl of Wiltshire is already there.

Bushy.   Thither will I with you, for little office
The hateful commons will perform for us,
Except like curs to tear us all to pieces.
Will you go along with us?

Bagot.   No, I will to Ireland to his Majesty.

         Farewell; if heart's presages be not vain,

         We three here part that ne'er shall meet again.

Bushy.   That's as York thrives to beat back Bolingbroke.

Green.   Alas, poor Duke, the task he undertakes

         Is numb'ring sands, and drinking oceans dry:

         Where one on his side fights, thousands will fly.

         Farewell at once, for once, for all, and ever.

Bushy.   Well, we may meet again.

Bagot.   I fear me, never.

        [Exeunt]

*[Enter Bolingbroke, Duke of Hereford,
and Northumberland with some soldiers]*

Bolingbroke.   How far is it, my lord, to Berkeley now?

Northumberland.   Believe me, noble lord,

I am a stranger here in Gloucestershire.

These high wild hills and rough uneven ways

Draws out our miles and makes them wearisome;

And yet your fair discourse hath been as sugar,

Making the hard way sweet and delectable.

But I bethink me what a weary way

From Ravenspurgh to Cotshall will be found

In Ross and Willoughby, wanting your company,

Which I protest hath very much beguiled

The tediousness and process of my travel:

But theirs is sweet'ned with the hope to have

The present benefit which I possess;

And hope to joy is little less in joy

Than hope enjoyed. By this the weary lords

Shall make their way seem short as mine hath done,

By sight of what I have, your noble company.

Bolingbroke. Of much less value is my company

Than your good words. But who comes here?

          [Enter Harry Percy]

Northumberland. It is my son, young Harry Percy,

Sent from my brother Worcester whencesoever.

Harry, how fares your uncle?

Percy. I had thought, my lord, to have learned his health of you.

Northumberland. Why, is he not with the Queen?

Percy. No, my good lord, he hath forsook the court,

Broken his staff of office, and dispersed

The household of the King.

Northumberland.   What was his reason?

He was not so resolved when last we spake together.

Percy.	Because your lordship was proclaimèd traitor;
	But he, my lord, is gone to Ravenspurgh
	To offer service to the Duke of Hereford,
	And sent me over by Berkeley to discover
	What power the Duke of York had levied there,
	Then with directions to repair to Ravenspurgh.
Northumberland.	Have you forgot the Duke of Hereford, boy?
Percy.	No, my good lord, for that is not forgot
	Which ne'er I did remember. To my knowledge
	I never in my life did look on him.
Northumberland.	Then learn to know him now—this is the Duke.
Percy.	My gracious lord, I tender you my service,
	Such as it is, being tender, raw, and young,
	Which elder days shall ripen and confirm
	To more approvèd service and desert.
Bolingbroke.	I thank thee, gentle Percy, and be sure
	I count myself in nothing else so happy

As in a soul rememb'ring my good friends;

And as my fortune ripens with thy love,

It shall be still thy true love's recompense:

My heart this covenant makes, my hand thus seals it.

Northumberland. How far is it to Berkeley, and what stir

Keeps good old York there with his men of war?

Percy. There stands the castle by yon tuft of trees,

Manned with three hundred men, as I have heard,

And in it are the Lords of York, Berkeley, and Seymour,

None else of name and noble estimate.

        [*Enter Ross and Willoughby*]

Northumberland. Here come the Lords of Ross and Willoughby,

Bloody with spurring, fiery red with haste.

Bolingbroke. Welcome, my lords, I wot your love pursues

A banished traitor. All my treasury

Is yet but unfelt thanks, which more enriched

Shall be your love and labor's recompense.

Ross. Your presence makes us rich, most noble lord.

Willoughby.	And far surmounts our labor to attain it.
Bolingbroke.	Evermore thank's the exchequer of the poor,
	Which till my infant fortune comes to years
	Stands for my bounty. But who comes here?

       [Enter Berkeley]

Northumberland.	It is my Lord of Berkeley, as I guess.
Berkeley.	My Lord of Hereford, my message is to you.
Bolingbroke.	My lord, my answer is—to Lancaster;
	And I am come to seek that name in England;
	And I must find that title in your tongue
	Before I make reply to aught you say.
Berkeley.	Mistake me not, my lord; 'tis not my meaning
	To race one title of your honor out.
	To you, my lord, I come—what lord you will—
	From the most gracious regent of this land,
	The Duke of York, to know what pricks you on
	To take advantage of the absent time,
	And fright our native peace with self-borne arms?

       [Enter York, attended]

Bolingbroke. I shall not need transport my words by you:

Here comes his Grace in person. My noble uncle!

[*Kneels*]

York. Show me thy humble heart, and not thy knee,

Whose duty is deceivable and false.

Bolingbroke. My gracious uncle—

York. Tut, tut! Grace me no grace, nor uncle me no uncle;

I am no traitor's uncle, and that word "grace"

In an ungracious mouth is but profane.

Why have those banished and forbidden legs

Dared once to touch a dust of England's ground?

But then, more "why?" Why have they dared to march

So many miles upon her peaceful bosom,

Frighting her pale-faced villages with war,

And ostentation of despisèd arms?

Com'st thou because the anointed King is hence?

Why, foolish boy, the King is left behind,

And in my loyal bosom lies his power.

Were I but now the lord of such hot youth

As when brave Gaunt, thy father, and myself

Rescued the Black Prince, that young Mars of men,

From forth the ranks of many thousand French,

O, then, how quickly should this arm of mine,

Now prisoner to the palsy, chastise thee,

And minister correction to thy fault!

Bolingbroke. My gracious uncle, let me know my fault:

On what condition stands it, and wherein?

York. Even in condition of the worst degree

In gross rebellion and detested treason.

Thou art a banished man, and here art come

Before the expiration of thy time,

In braving arms against thy sovereign.

Bolingbroke. As I was banished, I was banished Hereford,

But as I come, I come for Lancaster.

And, noble uncle, I beseech your Grace,

Look on my wrongs with an indifferent eye.

You are my father, for methinks in you

I see old Gaunt alive. O, then, my father,

Will you permit that I shall stand condemned,

A wandering vagabond, my rights and royalties
Plucked from my arms perforce, and given away
To upstart unthrifts? Wherefore was I born?
If that my cousin king be King in England,
It must be granted I am Duke of Lancaster.
You have a son, Aumerle, my noble cousin:
Had you first died, and he been thus trod down,
He should have found his uncle Gaunt a father,
To rouse his wrongs and chase them to the bay.
I am denied to sue my livery here,
And yet my letters patents give me leave.
My father's goods are all distrained and sold,
And these, and all, are all amiss employed.
What would you have me do? I am a subject;
And I challenge law, attorneys are denied me;
And therefore personally I lay my claim
To my inheritance of free descent.

Northumberland.	The noble Duke hath been too much abused.
Ross.	It stands your Grace upon to do him right.
Willoughby.	Base men by his endowments are made great.
York.	My lords of England, let me tell you this:
	I have had feeling of my cousin's wrongs,
	And labored all I could to do him right;
	But in this kind to come in braving arms,
	Be his own carver, and cut out his way,
	To find out right with wrong—it may not be:
	And you that do abet him in this kind
	Cherish rebellion, and are rebels all.
Northumberland.	The noble Duke hath sworn his coming is
	But for his own; and for the right of that
	We all have strongly sworn to give him aid:
	And let him never see joy that breaks that oath.

York. Well, well, I see the issue of these arms.

I cannot mend it, I must needs confess,

Because my power is weak and all ill left:

But if I could, by Him that gave me life,

I would attach you all, and make you stoop

Unto the sovereign mercy of the King.

But since I cannot, be it known unto you

I do remain as neuter. So fare you well—

Unless you please to enter in the castle,

And there repose you for this night.

Bolingbroke. An offer, uncle, that we will accept.

But we must win your grace to go with us

To Bristow Castle, which they say is held

By Bushy, Bagot, and their complices,

The caterpillars of the commonwealth,

Which I have sworn to weed and pluck away.

York. It may be I will go with you, but yet I'll pause,

For I am loath to break our country's laws.

Nor friends, nor foes, to me welcome you are.

Things past redress are now with me past care.

　　[Exeunt]

SCENE IV
IN WALES

[Enter Earl of Salisbury, and a Welsh Captain]

Captain. My Lord of Salisbury, we have stayed ten more days.

And hardly keep our countrymen together,

And yet we hear no tidings from the King;

Therefore we will disperse ourselves. Farewell.

Salisbury. Stay yet another day, thou trusty Welshman;

The King reposeth all his confidence in thee.

Captain. 'Tis thought the King is dead: we will not stay.

The bay trees in our country are all withered,

And meteors fright the fixèd stars of heaven,

The pale-faced moon looks bloody on the earth,

And lean-looked prophets whisper fearful change;

Rich men look sad, and ruffians dance and leap,

The one in fear to lose what they enjoy,

The other to enjoy by rage and war.

These signs forerun the death or fall of kings.

Farewell; our countrymen are gone and fled,

As well assured Richard their king is dead.

　　　　[*Exit*]

Salisbury.　Ah, Richard! With the eyes of heavy mind

I see thy glory like a shooting star

Fall to the base earth from the firmament;

Thy sun sets weeping in the lowly west,

Witnessing storms to come, woe and unrest;

Thy friends are fled to wait upon thy foes,

And crossly to thy good all fortune goes.

　　　　[*Exit*]

ACT THREE

[Enter Bolingbroke, Duke of Hereford, York, Northumber-
land, other Lords, Soldiers. Bushy and Green as prisoners]

Bolingbroke.   Bring forth these men.

Bushy and Green, I will not vex your souls,

Since presently your souls must part your bodies,

With too much urging your pernicious lives,

For 'twere no charity; yet, to wash your blood

From off my hands, here in the view of men,

I will unfold some causes of your deaths.

You have misled a prince, a royal king,

A happy gentleman in blood and lineaments,

By you unhappied and disfigured clean;

You have in manner with your sinful hours

Made a divorce betwixt his queen and him,

Broke the possession of a royal bed,

And stained the beauty of a fair queen's cheeks

With tears, drawn from her eyes by your foul wrongs.
Myself a prince, by fortune of my birth,
Near to the King in blood, and near in love
Till you did make him misinterpret me,
Have stooped my neck under your injuries,
And sighed my English breath in foreign clouds,
Eating the bitter bread of banishment,
Whilst you have fed upon my signories,
Disparked my parks, and felled my forest woods,
From my own windows torn my household coat,
Raced out my impresse, leaving me no sign,
Save men's opinions and my living blood,
To show the world I am a gentleman.
This and much more, much more than twice all this,
Condemns you to the death. See them delivered over
To execution and the hand of death.

Bushy. More welcome is the stroke of death to me

Than Bolingbroke to England. Lords, farewell.

Green. My comfort is that heaven will take our souls

And plague injustice with the pains of hell.

Bolingbroke. My Lord Northumberland, see them dispatched.

[Exeunt Northumberland with Bushy and Green]

Uncle, you say the Queen is at your house;

For God's sake, fairly let her be intreated.

Tell her I send to her my kind commends;

Take special care my greetings be delivered.

York. A gentleman of mine I have dispatched

With letters of your love to her at large.

Bolingbroke. Thanks, gentle uncle. Come, Lords, away

To fight with Glendower and his complices;

A while to work, and after holiday.

[Exeunt]

[Enter the King, Aumerle, the Bishop of
Carlisle, etc. Drums, flourish, and colors]

Richard. Barkloughly Castle call they this at hand?

Aumerle. Yea, my lord, How brooks your Grace the air

After your late tossing on the breaking seas?

Richard. Needs must I like it well. I weep for joy

To stand upon my kingdom once again.

Dear earth, I do salute thee with my hand,

Though rebels wound thee with their horses' hoofs.

As a long-parted mother with her child

Plays fondly with her tears and smiles in meeting,

So weeping, smiling, greet I thee, my earth,

And do thee favors with my royal hands.

Feed not thy sovereign's foe, my gentle earth,

Nor with thy sweets comfort his ravenous sense;

But let thy spiders, that suck up thy venom,

And heavy-gaited toads lie in their way,
Doing annoyance to the treacherous feet
Which with usurping steps do trample thee;
Yield stinging nettles to mine enemies;
And when they from thy bosom pluck a flower,
Guard it, I pray thee, with a lurking adder
Whose double tongue may with a mortal touch
Throw death upon thy sovereign's enemies.
Mock not my senseless conjuration, lords:
This earth shall have a feeling, and these stones
Prove armèd soldiers, ere her native king
Shall falter under foul rebellion's arms.

Carlisle. Fear not, my lord; that power that made you king
Hath power to keep you king in spite of all.
The means that heavens yield must be embraced
And not neglected. Else heaven would,
And we will not: heaven's offer we refuse,
The proffered means of succor and redress.

Aumerle. He means, my lord, that we are too remiss,

Whilst Bolingbroke through our security

Grows strong and great in substance and in power.

Richard. Discomfortable cousin, know'st thou not

That when the searching eye of heaven is hid

Behind the globe and lights the lower world,

Then thieves and robbers range abroad unseen

In murders and in outrage boldly here:

But when from under this terrestrial ball

He fires the proud tops of the eastern pines

And darts his light through every guilty hole,

Then murders, treasons, and detested sins,

The cloak of night being plucked from off their backs,

Stand bare and naked, trembling at themselves?

So when this thief, this traitor, Bolingbroke,

Who all this while hath reveled in the night

Whilst we were wand'ring with the Antipodes,

Shall see us rising in our throne, the east,

His treasons will sit blushing in his face,

Not able to endure the sight of day,

But self-affrighted tremble at his sin.

Not all the water in the rough rude sea

Can wash the balm off from an anointed king;

The breath of worldly men cannot depose

The deputy elected by the Lord.

For every man that Bolingbroke hath pressed

To lift shrewd steel against our golden crown,

God for his Richard hath in heavenly pay

A glorious angel; then, if angels fight,

Weak men must fall, for heaven still guards the right.

    [*Enter Salisbury*]

Welcome, my lord. How far off lies your power?

Salisbury.	Nor near, nor farther off, my gracious lord,
	Than this weak arm. Discomfort guides my tongue,
	And bids me speak of nothing but despair.
	One day too late, I fear me, noble lord,
	Hath clouded all thy happy days on earth.
	O, call back yesterday, bid time return,
	And thou shalt have twelve thousand fighting men.
	Today, today, unhappy day too late,
	O'erthrows thy joys, friends, fortune, and thy state;
	For all the Welshmen, hearing thou wert dead,
	Are gone to Bolingbroke, dispersed and fled.
Aumerle.	Comfort, my liege, why looks your Grace so pale?
Richard.	But now the blood of twenty thousand men
	Did triumph in my face, and they are fled;
	And till so much blood thither come again,
	Have I not reason to look pale and dead?
	All souls that will be safe fly from my side,
	For Time hath set a blot upon my pride.
Aumerle.	Comfort, my liege, remember who you are.

Richard.   I had forgot myself: am I not King?

Awake, thou coward majesty! Thou sleepest.

Is not the King's name twenty thousand names?

Arm, arm, my name! A puny subject strikes

At thy great glory. Look not to the ground,

Ye favorites of a king, are we not high?

High be our thoughts. I know my uncle York

Hath power enough to serve our turn. But who comes here?

[*Enter Scroop*]

Scroop.   More health and happiness betide my liege

Than can my care-tuned tongue deliver him.

Richard.   Mine ear is open, and my heart prepared;

The worst is worldly loss thou canst unfold.

Say, is my kingdom lost? Why, 'twas my care,

And what loss is it to be rid of care?

Strives Bolingbroke to be as great as we?

Greater he shall not be; if he serve God,

We'll serve Him too, and be his fellow so.

Revolt our subjects? That we cannot mend:

They break their faith to God as well as us.

Cry woe, destruction, ruin, and decay:

The worst is death, and death will have his day.

Scroop. Glad am I that your Highness is so armed

To bear the tidings of calamity.

Like an unseasonable stormy day

Which makes the silver rivers drown their shores

As if the world were all dissolved to tears,

So high above his limits swells the rage

Of Bolingbroke, covering your fearful land

With hard bright steel and hearts harder than steel.

White beards have armed their thin and hairless scalps

Against thy majesty; boys with women's voices

Strive to speak big, and clap their female joints

In stiff unwieldy arms against thy crown;

Thy very beadsmen learn to bend their bows

Of double-fatal yew against thy state;

Yea, distaff-women manage rusty bills

Against thy seat: both young and old rebel,

And all goes worse than I have power to tell.

Richard.	Too well, too well thou tell'st a tale so ill.
	Where is the Earl of Wiltshire? Where is Bagot?
	What is become of Bushy? Where is Green?
	That they have let the dangerous enemy
	Measure our confines with such peaceful steps?
	If we prevail, their heads shall pay for it.
	I warrant they have made peace with Bolingbroke.
Scroop.	Peace have they made with him indeed, my lord.
Richard.	O, villains, vipers, damned without redemption!
	Dogs easily won to fawn on any man!
	Snakes in my heart-blood warmed that sting my heart!
	Three Judases, each one thrice worse than Judas!
	Would they make peace? Terrible hell
	Make war upon their spotted souls for this!
Scroop.	Sweet love, I see, changing his property,
	Turns to the sourest and most deadly hate.
	Again uncurse their souls: their peace is made
	With heads and not with hands; those whom you curse
	Have felt the worst of death's destroying wound,
	And lie full low, graved in the hollow ground.

Aumerle.	Is Bushy, Green, and the Earl of Wiltshire dead?
Scroop.	Ay, all of them at Bristow lost their heads.
Aumerle.	Where is the Duke, my father, with his power?
Richard.	No matter where—of comfort no man speak.

Let's talk of graves, of worms, and epitaphs,
Make dust our paper, and with rainy eyes
Write sorrow on the bosom of the earth.
Let's choose executors and talk of wills:
And yet not so, for what can we bequeath
Save our deposèd bodies to the ground?
Our lands, our lives, and all are Bolingbroke's,
And nothing can we call our own, but death
And that small model of the barren earth
Which serves as paste and cover to our bones.
For God's sake let us sit upon the ground
And tell sad stories of the death of kings:
How some have been deposed, some slain in war,

Some haunted by the ghosts they have deposed,

Some poisoned by their wives, some sleeping killed,

All murdered—for within the hollow crown

That rounds the mortal temples of a king

Keeps Death his court, and their the antic sits,

Scoffing his state and grinning at his pomp,

Allowing him a breath, a little scene,

To monarchize, be feared, and kill with looks,

Infusing him with self and vain conceit,

As if this flesh which walls about our life

Were brass impregnable; and, humored thus,

Comes at the last, and with a little pin

Bores thorough his castle wall, and farewell king!

Cover your heads, and mock not flesh and blood

With solemn reverence; throw away respect,

Tradition, form, and ceremonious duty;

For you have but mistook me all this while:

I live with bread like you, feel want,

Taste grief, need friends—subjected thus,

How can you say to me, I am a king?

Carlisle. My lord, wise men ne'er sit and wail their woes,
But presently prevent the ways to wail.
To fear the foe, since fear oppresseth strength,
Gives in your weakness strength unto your foe;
And so your follies fight against yourself.
Fear and be slain, no worse can come to fight,
And fight and die is death destroying death,
Where fearing dying pays death servile breath.

Aumerle. My father hath a power; inquire of him,
And learn to make a body of a limb.

Richard. Thou chid'st me well. Proud Bolingbroke, I come
To change blows with thee for our day of doom.
This ague fit of fear is overblown;
An easy task it is to win our own.
Say, Scroop, where lies our uncle with his power?
Speak sweetly, man, although thy looks be sour.

Scroop. Men judge by the complexion of the sky

The state and inclination of the day;

So may you by my dull and heavy eye.

My tongue hath but a heavier tale to say.

I play the torturer by small and small

To lengthen out the worst that must be spoken:

Your uncle York is joined with Bolingbroke,

And all your northern castles yielded up,

And all your southern gentlemen in arms

Upon his party.

Richard.   Thou hast said enough.

Beshrew thee, cousin, which didst lead me forth

Of that sweet way I was in to despair.

What say you now? What comfort have we now?

By heaven, I'll hate him everlastingly

That bids me be of comfort any more.

Go to Flint Castle: there I'll pine away;

A king, woe's slave, shall kingly woe obey.

That power I have, discharge, and let them go

To ear the land that hath some hope to grow,

For I have none. Let no man speak again

To alter this, for counsel is but vain.

Aumerle. My liege, one word.

Richard.   He does me double wrong

That wounds me with the flatteries of his tongue.

Discharge my followers, let them hence away,

From Richard's night to Bolingbroke's fair day.

[*Exeunt*]

[*Enters with a drum and colors: Bolingbroke,*
York, Northumberland, Attendants and Soldiers]

Bolingbroke. So that by this intelligence we learn

The Welshmen are dispersed, and Salisbury

Is gone to meet the King, who lately landed

With some few private friends upon this coast.

Northumberland. The news is very fair and good, my lord;

Richard not far from hence hath hid his head.

York. It would beseem the Lord Northumberland

To say "King Richard." Alack, the heavy day

When such a sacred king should hide his head.

Northumberland. Your Grace mistakes; only to be brief

Left I his title out.

York.   The time hath been

Would you have been so brief with him, he would

Have been so brief with you to shorten you,

For taking so the head, your whole head's length.

Bolingbroke. Mistake not, uncle, further than you should.

York. Take not, good cousin, further than you should,

Lest you mis-take: the heavens are over our heads.

Bolingbroke. I know it, uncle, and oppose not myself

Against their will. But who comes here?

[*Enter Percy*]

Welcome, Harry. What, will not this castle yield?

Percy. The castle royally is manned, my lord,

Against thy entrance.

Bolingbroke. Royally!

Why, it contains no king?

Percy. Yes, my good lord,

It doth contain a king: King Richard lies

Within the limits of yon lime and stone;

And with him are the Lord Aumerle, Lord Salisbury,

Sir Stephen Scroop, besides a clergyman

Of holy reverence—who, I cannot learn.

Northumberland. O, belike it is the Bishop of Carlisle.

Bolingbroke.   Noble lord,
Go to the rude ribs of that ancient castle,
Through brazen trumpet send the breath of parley
Into his ruined ears, and thus deliver:
Henry Bolingbroke
On both his knees doth kiss King Richard's hand,
And sends allegiance and true faith of heart
To his most royal person; hither come
Even at his feet to lay my arms and power,
Provided that my banishment repealed,
And lands restored again be freely granted;
If not, I'll use the advantage of my power,
And lay the summer's dust with showers of blood
Rained from the wounds of slaughtered Englishmen—
The which, how far off from the mind of Bolingbroke
It is such crimson tempest should bedrench
The fresh green lap of fair King Richard's land,
My stooping duty tenderly shall show.
Go, signify as much, while here we march
Upon the grassy carpet of this plain.

Let's march without the noise of threat'ning drum,

That from this castle's tattered battlements

Our fair appointments may be well perused.

Methinks King Richard and myself should meet

With no less terror than the elements

Of fire and water, when their thund'ring shock

At meeting tears the cloudy cheeks of heaven.

Be he the fire, I'll be the yielding water;

The rage be his, whilst on the earth I rain

My waters—on the earth, and not on him.

March on, and mark King Richard how he looks.

*[The trumpets sound parle without, and answer within;
then a flourish. Richard appeareth on the walls with
the Bishop of Carlisle, Aumerle, Scroop, Salisbury]*

See, see King Richard doth himself appear,

As doth the blushing discontented sun

From out the fiery portal of the East,

When he perceives the envious clouds are bent

To dim his glory, and to stain the track

Of his bright passage to the Occident.

York.   Yet looks he like a king: behold his eye,

          As bright as is the eagle's, lightens forth

          Controlling majesty. Alack, alack for woe,

          That any harm should stain so fair a show.

Richard.   [*To Northumberland*] We are amazed, and thus long have we stood

          To watch the fearful bending of thy knee,

          Because we thought ourself thy lawful king:

          And if we be, how dare thy joints forget

          To pay their awful duty to our presence?

          If we be not, show us the hand of God

          That hath dismissed us from our stewardship;

          For well we know no hand of blood and bone

          Can gripe the sacred handle of our scepter,

          Unless he do profane, steal, or usurp;

          And though you think that all, as you have done,

          Have torn their souls by turning them from us,

          And we are barren and bereft of friends,

          Yet know, my master, God omnipotent,

Is mustering in his clouds on our behalf

Armies of pestilence, and they shall strike

Your children yet unborn and unbegot

That lift your vassal hands against my head,

And threat the glory of my precious crown.

Tell Bolingbroke—for yon methinks he stands—

That every stride he makes upon my land

Is dangerous treason. He is come to open

The purple testament of bleeding war;

But ere the crown he looks for live in peace

Ten thousand bloody crowns of mothers' sons

Shall ill become the flower of England's face,

Change the complexion of her maid-pale peace

To scarlet indignation, and bedew

Her pastor's grass with faithful English blood.

Northumberland. The King of heaven forbid our lord the King

Should so with civil and uncivil arms

Be rushed upon. Thy thrice-noble cousin,

Harry Bolingbroke, doth humbly kiss thy hand,

And by the honorable tomb he swears

That stands upon your royal grandshire's bones,
And by the royalties of both your bloods—
Currents that spring from one most gracious head—
And by the buried hand of warlike Gaunt,
And by the worth and honor of himself,
Comprising all that may be sworn or said,
His coming hither hath no further scope
Than for his lineal royalties, and to beg
Infranchisement immediate on his knees;
Which on thy royal party granted once,
His glittering arms he will commend to rust,
His barbèd steeds to stables, and his heart
To faithful service of your Majesty.
This swears he, as he is a prince and just;
And, as I am a gentleman, I credit him.

Richard. Northumberland, say thus the King returns,
His noble cousin is right welcome hither,
And all the number of his fair demands
Shall be accomplished without contradiction.
With all the gracious utterance thou hast
Speak to his gentle hearing kind commends.
[*To Aumerle*] We do debase ourselves, cousin, do we not,
To look so poorly and to speak so fair?
Shall we call back Northumberland, and send
Defiance to the traitor and so die?

Aumerle. No, good my lord; let's fight with gentle words,
Till time lend friends, and friends their helpful swords.

Richard. O God! O God! That e'er this tongue of mine,
That laid the sentence of dread banishment
On yon proud man, should take it off again
With words of sooth! O, that I were as great
As is my grief, or lesser than my name!
Or that I could forget what I have been!

Or not remember what I must be now!

Swell'st thou, proud heart? I'll give thee scope to beat,

Since foes have scope to beat both thee and me.

Aumerle. Northumberland comes back from Bolingbroke.

Richard. What must the King do now? Must he submit?

The King shall do it. Must he be deposed?

The King shall be contented. Must he lose

The name of king? A God's name, let it go.

I'll give my jewels for a set of beads;

My gorgeous palace for a hermitage;

My gay apparel for an almsman's gown;

My figured goblets for a dish of wood;

My scepter for a palmer's walking-staff;

My subjects for a pair of carvèd saints;

And my large kingdom for a little grave,

A little, little grave, an obscure grave;

Or I'll be buried in the King's highway,

Some way of common trade, where subject's feet

May hourly trample on their sovereign's head;

For on my heart they tread now whilst I live,
And buried once, why not upon my head?
Aumerle, thou weep'st, my tender-hearted cousin:
We'll make foul weather with despisèd tears;
Our sighs and they shall lodge the summer corn,
And make a dearth in this revolting land:
Or shall we play the wantons with our woes
And make some pretty match with shedding tears,
As thus, to drop them still upon one place,
Till they have fretted us a pair of graves
Within the earth; and, therein laid, "there lies
Two kinsmen digged their graves with weeping eyes":
Would not this ill do well? Well, well, I see
I talk but idly, and you laugh at me.
Most mighty prince, my Lord Northumberland,
What says King Bolingbroke? Will his Majesty
Give Richard leave to live till Richard die?
You make a leg, and Bolingbroke says "Ay."

Northumberland. My lord, in the base court he doth attend

To speak with you; may it please you to come down?

Richard. Down, down I come, like glist'ring Phaethon,

Wanting the manage of unruly jades.

In the base court! Base court where kings grow base,

To come at traitors' calls, and do them grace:

In the base court, come down: down court, down king,

For night owls shriek where mounting larks should sing.

Bolingbroke. What says his Majesty?

Northumberland.   Sorrow, and grief of heart

Makes him speak fondly like a frantic man;

Yet he is come.

[Enter King Richard and Attendants, below]

Bolingbroke.   Stand all apart,

And show fair duty to his Majesty.

[He kneels down]

My gracious Lord.

Richard. Fair cousin, you debase your princely knee

To make the base earth proud with kissing it.

Me rather had my heart might feel your love,

Than my unpleased eye see your courtesy.

Up, cousin, up, your heart is up, I know,

Thus high at least, although your knee be low.

Bolingbroke. My gracious lord, I come but for mine own.

Richard. Your own is yours, and I am yours, and all.

Bolingbroke. So far be mine, my most redoubted lord,

As my true service shall deserve your love.

Richard. Well you deserve: they well deserve to have

That know the strong'st and surest way to get.

Uncle, give me your hands; nay, dry your eyes;

Tears show their love, but want their remedies.

Cousin, I am too young to be your father,

Though you are old enough to be my heir.

What you will have, I'll give, and willing too,

For do we must what force will have us do.

Set on towards London, cousin, is it so?

Bolingbroke. Yea, my good Lord.

Richard.   Then I must not say no.

{*Flourish. Exeunt*}

*[Enter the Queen with two
Ladies, and her attendants]*

Queen. What sport shall we devise here in this garden,

To drive away the heavy thought of care?

Lady. Madame, we'll play at bowls.

Queen. 'Twill make me think the world is full of rubs,

And that my fortune runs against the bias.

Lady. Madame, we'll dance.

Queen. My legs can keep no measure in delight,

When my poor heart no measure keeps in grief:

Therefore no dancing, girl; some other sport.

Lady. Madame, we'll tell tales.

Queen. Of sorrow, or of joy?

Lady.   Of either, madame.

Queen. Of neither, girl.

For if of joy, being altogether wanting,

It doth remember me the more of sorrow;

Or if of grief, being altogether had,

It adds more sorrow to my want of joy:

For what I have I need not to repeat,

And what I want it boots not to complain.

Lady. Madame, I'll sing.

Queen.   'Tis well that thou hast cause;

But thou should'st please me better, would'st thou weep.

Lady. I could weep, madame, would it do you good.

Queen. And I could sing, would weeping do me good,

And never borrow any tear of thee.

        [*Enter Gardeners. One the master, the other two his men*]

But stay, here come the gardeners.

Let's step into the shadow of these trees.

My wretchedness unto a row of pins,

They will talk of state, for every one doth so

Against a change; woe is forerun with woe.

Gardener. [*To one Servant*] Go, bind thou up young dangling apricocks,

Which like unruly children make their sire

Stoop with oppression of their prodigal weight;

Give some supportance to the bending twigs.

[*To the other*] Go thou, and like an executioner

Cut off the heads of too fast growing sprays

That look too lofty in our commonwealth:

All must be even in our government.

You thus employed, I will go root away

The noisome weeds which without profit suck

The soil's fertility from wholesome flowers.

Man. Why should we, in the compass of a pale,

Keep law and form and due proportion,

Showing, as in a model, our firm estate,

When our sea-wallèd garden, the whole land,

Is full of weeds, her fairest flowers choked up,

Her fruit trees all unpruned, her hedges ruined,

Her knots disordered, and her wholesome herbs

Swarming with caterpillars?

Gardener.   Hold thy peace.
He that hath suffered this disordered spring
Hath now himself met with the fall of leaf:
The weeds which his broad spreading leaves did shelter,
That seemed in eating him to hold him up,
Are plucked up root and all by Bolingbroke—
I mean the Earl of Wiltshire, Bushy, Green.

Man.   What, are they dead?

Gardener.   They are; and Bolingbroke
Hath seized the wasteful King. O, what pity is it
That he had not so trimmed and dressed his land
As we this garden! We at time of year
Do wound the bark, the skin of our fruit trees,
Lest being overproud in sap and blood
With too much riches it confound itself;
Had he done so to great and growing men,

They might have lived to bear, and he to taste

Their fruits of duty. Superfluous branches

We lop away, that bearing boughs may live: ·

Had he done so, himself had borne the crown,

Which waste of idle hours hath quite thrown down.

Man. What, think you the King shall be deposed?

Gardener. Depressed he is already, and deposed

'Tis doubt he will be. Letters came last night

To a dear friend of the good Duke of York's,

That tell black tidings.

Queen. O, I am pressed to death

Through want of speaking!

    [Comes forward]

Thou, old Adam's likeness, set to dress this garden,

How dares thy harsh rude tongue sound this unpleasing news?

What Eve, what serpent hath suggested thee

To make a second fall of cursèd man?

Why dost thou say King Richard is deposed?
Dar'st thou, thou little better thing than earth,
Divine his downfall? Say, where, when and how
Cam'st thou by this ill tidings? Speak, thou wretch.

Gardener. Pardon me, madame; little joy have I
To breathe this news, yet what I say is true:
King Richard he is in the mighty hold
Of Bolingbroke. Their fortunes both are weighed:
In your lord's scale is nothing but himself
And some few vanities that make him light;
But in the balance of great Bolingbroke
Besides himself are all the English peers,
And with that odds he weighs King Richard down.
Post you to London, and you will find it so;
I speak no more than everyone doth know.

Queen. Nimble mischance, that art so light of foot,

Doth not thy embassage belong to me,

And am I last that knows it? O, thou thinkest

To serve me last that I may longest keep

Thy sorrow in my breast! Come, ladies, go

To meet at London London's king in woe.

What, was I born to this, that my sad look

Should grace the triumph of great Bolingbroke?

Gard'ner, for telling me these news of woe,

Pray God, the plants thou graft'st may never grow.

[*Exit with Ladies*]

Gardener. Poor queen, so that thy state might be no worse,

I would my skill were subject to thy curse.

Here did she fall a tear; here in this place

I'll set a bank of rue, sour herb of grace;

Rue even for ruth here shortly shall be seen,

In the remembrance of a weeping queen.

[*Exeunt*]

ACT FOUR

[Enter Bolingbroke, with the Lords Aumerle,
Northumberland, Percy, Fitzwater, Surrey, the
Bishop of Carlisle, the Abbot of Westminster,
another Lord, Herald, and Officers to Parliament]

Bolingbroke. Call forth Bagot.

       [Enter Bagot with Officers]

Now, Bagot, freely speak thy mind,

What thou dost know of noble Gloucester's death,

Who wrought it with the King, and who performed

The bloody office of his timeless end.

Bagot. Then set before my face the Lord Aumerle.

Bolingbroke. Cousin, stand forth, and look upon that man.

Bagot. My Lord Aumerle, I know your daring tongue

Scorns to unsay what once it hath delivered.

In that dead time when Gloucester's death was plotted,

I heard you say, "Is not my arm of length,
That reacheth from the restful English court
As far as Callice to mine uncle's head?"
Amongst much other talk that very time
I heard you say that you had rather refuse
The offer of an hundred thousand crowns
Than Bolingbroke's return to England;
Adding withal, how blest this land would be
In this your cousin's death.

Aumerle.   Princes and noble Lords,
What answer shall I make to this base man?
Shall I so much dishonor my fair stars
On equal terms to give him chastisement?
Either I must, or have mine honor soiled
With the attainder of his slanderous lips.
There is my gage, the manual seal of death,
That marks thee out for hell: I say thou liest,
And will maintain what thou hast said is false
In thy heart-blood, though being all too base
To stain the temper of my knightly sword.

Bolingbroke.	Bagot, forbear, thou shalt not take it up.
Aumerle.	Excepting one, I would he were the best
	In all this presence that hath moved me so.
Fitzwater.	If that thy valor stand on sympathy,
	There is my gage, Aumerle, in gage to thine;
	By that fair sun which shows me where thou stand'st,
	I heard thee say, and vauntingly thou spak'st it,
	That thou wert cause of noble Gloucester's death.
	If thou deniest it twenty times, thou liest,
	And I will turn thy falsehood to thy heart,
	Where it was forgèd, with my rapier's point.
Aumerle.	Thou dar'st not, coward, live to see that day.
Fitzwater.	Now, by my soul, I would it were this hour!
Aumerle.	Fitzwater, thou art damned to hell for this.

Percy. Aumerle, thou liest, his honor is as true

In this appeal as thou are all unjust;

And that thou art so, there I throw my gage,

To prove it on thee to the extremest point

Of mortal breathing; seize it if thou dar'st.

Aumerle. And if I do not, may my hands rot off,

And never brandish more revengeful steel

Over the glittering helmet of my foe.

Another Lord. I task the earth to the like, forsworn Aumerle,

And spur thee on with full as many lies

As may be hollowed in thy treacherous ear

From sun to sun: there is my honor's pawn;

Engage it to the trial if thou darest.

Aumerle. Who sets me else? By heaven, I'll throw at all!

I have a thousand spirits in one breast

To answer twenty thousand such as you.

Surrey.	My Lord Fitzwater, I do remember well
	The very time Aumerle and you did talk.
Fitzwater.	'Tis very true; you were in presence then,
	And you can witness with me this is true.
Surrey.	As false, by heaven, as heaven itself is true!
Fitzwater.	Surrey, thou liest.
Surrey.	Dishonorable boy,
	That lie shall lie so heavy on my sword,
	That it shall render vengeance and revenge,
	Till thou, the lie-giver, and that lie do lie
	In earth as quiet as thy father's skull.
	In proof whereof, there is my honor's pawn;
	Engage it to the trial if thou dar'st.

Fitzwater.	How fondly dost thou spur a forward horse!
	If I dare eat, or drink, or breathe, or live,
	I dare meet Surrey in a wilderness,
	And spit upon him, whilst I say he lies,
	And lies, and lies. There is my bond of faith,
	To tie thee to my strong correction.
	As I intend to thrive in this new world,
	Aumerle is guilty of my true appeal.
	Besides, I heard the banished Norfolk say
	That thou, Aumerle, did'st send two of thy men
	To execute the noble Duke at Callice.
Aumerle.	Some honest Christian trust me with a gage.
	That Norfolk lies, here do I throw down this,
	If he may be repealed to try his honor.

Bolingbroke. These differences shall all rest under gage
Till Norfolk be repealed; repealed he shall be,
And, though mine enemy, restored again
To all his lands and signories. When he is returned,
Against Aumerle we will inforce his trial.

Carlisle. That honorable day shall never be seen.
Many a time hath banished Norfolk fought
For Jesu Christ in glorious Christian field,
Streaming the ensign of the Christian cross
Against black pagans, Turks, and Saracens;
And, toiled with works of war, retired himself
To Italy, and there at Venice gave
His body to that pleasant country's earth,
And his pure soul unto his captain, Christ,
Under whose colors he had fought so long.

Bolingbroke.	Why, Bishop, is Norfolk dead?
Carlisle.	As surely as I live, my lord.
Bolingbroke.	Sweet peace conduct his sweet soul to the bosom
	Of good old Abraham! Lords appellants,
	Your differences shall all rest under gage,
	Till we assign you to your days of trial.

               [Enter York]

York.	Great Duke of Lancaster, I come to thee
	From plume-plucked Richard, who with willing soul
	Adopts thee heir, and his high scepter yields
	To the possession of thy royal hand.
	Ascend his throne, descending now from him,
	And long live Henry, fourth of that name!
Bolingbroke.	In God's name, I'll ascend the regal throne.

Carlisle. Marry, God forbid!

Worst in this royal presence may I speak,

Yet best beseeming me to speak the truth.

Would God that any in this noble presence

Were enough noble to be upright judge

Of noble Richard. Then true noblesse would

Learn him forbearance from so foul a wrong.

What subject can give sentence on his king?

And who sits here that is not Richard's subject?

Thieves are not judged, but they are by to hear,

Although apparent guilt be seen in them;

And shall the figure of God's majesty,

His captain, steward, deputy elect,

Anointed, crownèd, planted many years,

Be judged by subject and inferior breath,

And he himself not present? O, forfend it, God,

That in a Christian climate souls refined

Should show so heinous, black, obscene a deed!

I speak to subjects and a subject speaks,

Stirred up by God thus boldly for his king.

My Lord of Hereford here, whom you call king,

Is a foul traitor to proud Hereford's king;

And if you crown him, let me prophesy

The blood of English shall manure the ground,

And future ages groan for this foul act;

Peace shall go sleep with Turks and infidels,

And, in this seat of peace, tumultuous wars

Shall kin with kin, and kind with kind, confound;

Disorder, horror, fear, and mutiny

Shall here inhabit, and this land be called

The field of Golgotha and dead men's skulls.

O, if you raise this house against this house,

It will the woefullest division prove

That ever fell upon this cursèd earth!

Prevent it, resist it, let it not be so,

Lest child, child's children, cry against you woe.

Northumberland. Well have you argued, sir; and for your pains

Of capital treason we arrest you here.

My Lord of Westminster, be it your charge

To keep him safely till his day of trial.

May it please you, lords, to grant the Commons' suit?

Bolingbroke. Fetch hither Richard, that in common view

He may surrender; so we shall proceed

Without suspicion.

York.   I will be his conduct.

[*Exit*]

Bolingbroke. Lords, you that here are under our arrest,

Procure your sureties for your days of answer.

Little are we beholding to your love,

And little looked for at your helping hands.

[*Enter Richard and York*]

Richard.   Alack, why am I sent for to a king,

Before I have shook off the regal thoughts

Wherewith I reigned? I hardly yet have learned

To insinuate, flatter, bow, and bend my knee.

Give Sorrow leave a while to tutor me

To this submission. Yet I well remember

The favors of these men: were they not mine?

Did they not sometime cry "All hail!" to me?

So Judas did to Christ: but he in twelve

Found truth in all but one; I, in twelve thousand, none.

God save the King! Will no man say "Amen"?

Am I both priest and clerk? Well, then, amen.

God save the King, although I be not he;

And yet amen, if heaven do think him me.

To do what service am I sent for hither?

York. To do that office of thine own good will,
Which tired majesty did make thee offer:
The resignation of thy state and crown
To Henry Bolingbroke.

Richard.   Give me the crown.
Here, cousin, seize the crown. Here, cousin,
On this side my hand, and on that side yours.
Now is this golden crown like a deep well
That owes two buckets, filling one another,
The emptier ever dancing in the air,
The other down, unseen, and full of water.
That bucket down and full of tears am I,
Drinking my griefs, whilst you mount up on high.

Bolingbroke. I thought you had been willing to resign.

Richard. My crown I am, but still my griefs are mine:
You may my glories and my state depose,
But not my griefs; still am I King of those.

Bolingbroke. Part of your cares you give me with your crown.

Richard.   Your cares set up, do not pluck my cares down.

My care is loss of care, by old care done;

Your care is gain of care, by new care won.

The cares I give, I have, though given away;

They 'tend the crown, yet still with me they stay.

Bolingbroke.   Are you contented to resign the crown?

Richard.   Ay, no; no, ay: for I must nothing be.

Therefore no, no, for I resign to thee.

Now, mark me how I will undo myself.

I give this heavy weight from off my head,

And this unwieldy scepter from my hand,

The pride of kingly sway from out my heart;

With mine own tears I wash away my balm,

With mine own hands I give away my crown,

With mine own tongue deny my sacred state,

With mine own breath release all duteous oaths;

All pomp and majesty I do forswear;

My manors, rents, revenues, I forgo;

My acts, decrees, and statutes I deny:

God pardon all oaths that are broke to me,

God keep all vows unbroke are made to thee.

Make me, that nothing have, with nothing grieved,

And thou with all pleased, that hast all achieved.

Long may'st thou live in Richard's seat to sit,

And soon lie Richard in an earthy pit.

God save King Henry, unkinged Richard says,

And send him many years of sunshine days.

What more remains?

Northumberland.   No more, but that you read

These accusations, and these grievous crimes,

Committed by your person and your followers,

Against the state and profit of this land:

That by confessing them, the souls of men

May deem that you are worthily deposed.

Richard. Must I do so? And must I ravel out
My weaved-up follies? Gentle Northumberland,
If thy offenses were upon record,
Would it not shame thee, in so fair a troop,
To read a lecture of them? If thou would'st,
There should'st thou find one heinous article,
Containing the deposing of a king,
And cracking the strong warrant of an oath,
Marked with a blot, damned in the book of heaven.
Nay, all of you that stand and look upon me,
Whilst that my wretchedness doth bait myself,
Though some of you, with Pilate, wash your hands,
Showing an outward pity: yet you Pilates
Have here delivered me to my sour cross,
And water cannot wash away your sin.

Northumberland. My lord, dispatch, read o'er these articles.

Richard. Mine eyes are full of tears, I cannot see:
And yet salt water blinds them not so much,
But they can see a sort of traitors here.
Nay, if I turn mine eyes upon myself,

I find myself a traitor with the rest;

For I have given here my soul's consent

T' undeck the pompous body of a king;

Made glory base, and sovereignty a slave,

Proud majesty a subject, state a peasant.

Northumberland. My lord—

Richard. No lord of thine, thou haught, insulting man,

Nor no man's lord: I have no name, no title,

No, not that name was given me at the font

But 'tis usurped. Alack, the heavy day!

That I have worn so many winters out,

And know not now what name to call myself.

O, that I were a mockery king of snow,

Standing before the sun of Bolingbroke,

To melt myself away in water drops!

Good king, great king—and yet not greatly good—

And if my word be sterling yet in England,

Let it command a mirror hither straight,

That it may show me what a face I have,

Since it is bankrout of his majesty.

Bolingbroke.	Go some of you, and fetch a looking glass.
	[Exit Attendant]
Northumberland.	Read o'er this paper while the glass doth come.
Richard.	Fiend, thou torments me, ere I come to hell.
Bolingbroke.	Urge it no more, my Lord Northumberland.
Northumberland.	The Commons will not then be satisfied.
Richard.	They shall be satisfied: I'll read enough,
	When I do see the very book indeed,
	Where all my sins are writ, and that's myself.
	[Enter one with a glass]
	Give me the glass, and therein will I read.
	No deeper wrinkles yet? Hath Sorrow struck
	So many blows upon this face of mine,
	And made no deeper wounds? O, flatt'ring glass!
	Like to my followers in prosperity,
	Thou dost beguile me. Was this face the face
	That every day under his household roof
	Did keep ten thousand men? Was this the face
	That, like the sun, did make beholders wink?

Was this the face that faced so many follies,
And was at last outfaced by Bolingbroke?
A brittle glory shineth in this face,
As brittle as the glory is the face,

[*Throws glass down*]

For there it is, cracked in a hundred shivers.
Mark, silent king, the moral of this sport:
How soon my sorrow hath destroyed my face.

Bolingbroke.   The shadow of your sorrow hath destroyed
The shadow of your face.

Richard.   Say that again.
"The shadow of my sorrow"? Ha, let's see.
'Tis very true, my grief lies all within,
And these external manners of laments
Are merely shadows to the unseen grief
That swells with silence in the tortured soul.
There lies the substance: and I thank thee, King,
For thy great bounty, that not only giv'st
Me cause to wail, but teachest me the way
How to lament the cause. I'll beg one boon,

And then be gone, and trouble you no more.

Shall I obtain it?

Bolingbroke.   Name it, fair cousin.

Richard.   Fair cousin? I am greater than a king:

For when I was a king, my flatterers

Were then but subjects; being now a subject,

I have a king here to my flatterer.

Being so great, I have no need to beg.

Bolingbroke.   Yet ask.

Richard.   And shall I have?

Bolingbroke.   You shall.

Richard.   Then give me leave to go.

Bolingbroke.   Whither?

Richard.   Whither you will, so I were from your sights.

Bolingbroke.   Go some of you, convey him to the Tower.

Richard.   O, good! "Convey"! Conveyers are you all,

That rise thus nimbly by a true king's fall.

{Exeunt Richard, some Lords, and Guards]

Bolingbroke. On Wednesday next we solemnly set down.

Our coronation: Lords, prepare yourselves.

[Exeunt. Manent the Abbot of West-
minster, Bishop of Carlisle, Aumerle]

Abbot. A woeful pageant have we here beheld.

Carlisle. The woe's to come; the children yet unborn

Shall feel this day as sharp to them as thorn.

Aumerle. You holy clergymen, is there no plot

To rid the realm of this pernicious blot?

Abbot. My lord,

Before I freely speak my mind herein,

You shall not only take the sacrament

To bury mine intents, but also to effect

Whatever I shall happen to devise.

I see your brows are full of discontent,

Your hearts of sorrow, and your eyes of tears.

Come home with me to supper: I will lay

A plot shall show us all a merry day.

[Exeunt]

ACT FIVE

[*Enter the Queen with her Attendants*]

Queen. This way the King will come, this is the way

To Julius Caesar's ill-erected Tower,

To whose flint bosom my condemnèd lord

Is doomed a prisoner by proud Bolingbroke.

Here let us rest, if this rebellious earth

Have any resting for her true king's queen.

[*Enter Richard and Guard*]

But soft, but see, or rather do not see

My fair rose wither; yet look up, behold,

That you in pity may dissolve to dew,

And wash him fresh again with true-love tears.

Ah, thou the model where old Troy did stand!

Thou map of honor, thou King Richard's tomb,

And not King Richard, thou most beauteous inn,

Why should hard-favored grief be lodged in thee,

When triumph is become an alehouse guest?

Richard. Join not with grief, fair woman, do not so,

To make my end too sudden; learn, good soul,

To think our former state a happy dream,

From which awaked, the truth of what we are

Shows us but this: I am sworn brother, sweet,

To grim Necessity, and he and I

Will keep a league till death. Hie thee to France,

And cloister thee in some religious house:

Our holy lives must win a new world's crown,

Which our profane hours here have stricken down.

Queen. What! Is my Richard both in shape and mind

Transformed and weakened? Hath Bolingbroke

Deposed thine intellect? Hath he been in thy heart?

The lion dying thrusteth forth his paw

And wounds the earth, if nothing else, with rage

To be o'erpow'red, and wilt thou, pupil-like,

Take the correction mildly, kiss the rod,

And fawn on Rage with base humility,

Which art a lion and the king of beasts?

Richard.   A king of beasts indeed: if aught but beasts,

I had been still a happy king of men.

Good sometimes queen, prepare thee hence for France.

Think I am dead, and that even here thou takest

As from my deathbed thy last living leave.

In winter's tedious nights sit by the fire

With good old folks, and let them tell thee tales

Of woeful ages long ago betid;

And ere thou bid good night, to quite their griefs

Tell thou the lamentable tale of me,

And send the hearers weeping to their beds.

For why, the senseless brands will sympathize

The heavy accent of thy moving tongue,

And in compassion weep the fire out:

And some will mourn in ashes, some coal-black,

For the deposing of a rightful king.

       [Enter Northumberland]

Northumberland. My lord, the mind of Bolingbroke is changed:

You must to Pomfret, not unto the Tower.

And, madam, there is order ta'en for you:

With all swift speed you must away to France.

Richard. Northumberland, thou ladder wherewithal

The mounting Bolingbroke ascends my throne,

The time shall not be many hours of age

More than it is, ere foul sin, gathering head,

Shall break into corruption. Thou shalt think,

Though he divide the realm and give thee half,

It is too little, helping him to all;

He shall think that thou which knowest the way

To plant unrightful kings, wilt know again,

Being ne'er so little urged another way,

To pluck him headlong from the usurped throne.

The love of wicked men converts to fear,

That fear to hate, and hate turns one or both

To worthy danger and deservèd death.

Northumberland.	My guilt be on my head, and there an end.
	Take leave and part, for you must part forthwith.
Richard.	Doubly divorced! Bad men, you violate
	A twofold marriage: 'twixt my crown and me,
	And then betwixt me and my married wife.
	Let me unkiss the oath 'twixt thee and me—
	And yet not so, for with a kiss 'twas made.
	Part us, Northumberland; I towards the north,
	Where shivering cold and sickness pines the clime;
	My wife to France, from whence, set forth in pomp,
	She came adornèd hither like sweet May,
	Sent back like Hallowmas, or short'st of day.
Queen.	And must we be divided? Must we part?
Richard.	Ay, hand from hand, my love, and heart from heart.
Queen.	Banish us both, and send the King with me.
Richard.	That were some love, but little policy.
Queen.	Then whither he goes, thither let me go.

Richard. So two together weeping make one woe.

Weep thou for me in France, I for thee here;

Better far off than, near, be ne'er the near.

Go count thy way with sighs, I mine with groans.

Queen. So longest way shall have the longest moans.

Richard. Twice for one step I'll groan, the way being short,

And piece the way out with a heavy heart.

Come, come, in wooing sorrow, let's be brief,

Since, wedding it, there is such length in grief.

One kiss shall stop our mouths, and dumbly part:

Thus give I mine, and thus take I thy heart.

Queen. Give me mine own again, 'twere no good part

To take on me to keep and kill thy heart.

So now I have mine own again, be gone,

That I may strive to kill it with a groan.

Richard. We make woe wanton with this fond delay:

Once more adieu, the rest let sorrow say.

            [*Exeunt, different ways*]

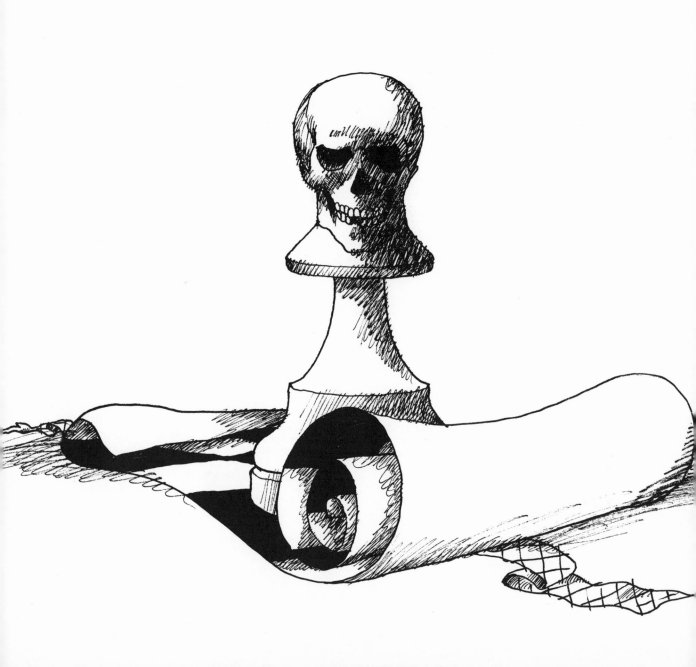

[Enter Duke of York and the Duchess]

Duchess. My lord, you told me you would tell the rest,

When weeping made you break the story off,

Of our two cousins' coming into London.

York. Where did I leave?

Duchess.   At that sad stop, my lord,

Where rude misgoverned hands from windows' tops

Threw dust and rubbish on King Richard's head.

York. Then, as I said, the Duke, great Bolingbroke,

Mounted upon a hot and fiery steed,

Which his aspiring rider seemed to know,

With slow but stately pace kept on his course,

Whilst all tongues cried "God save thee, Bolingbroke!"

You would have thought the very windows spake:

So many greedy looks of young and old

Through casements darted their desiring eyes

Upon his visage; and that all the walls

With painted imagery had said at once,
"Jesu preserve thee! Welcome, Bolingbroke!"
Whilst he, from the one side to the other turning,
Bareheaded, lower than his proud steed's neck,
Bespake them thus: "I thank you, countrymen."
And thus still doing, thus he passed along.

Duchess. Alack, poor Richard! Where rode he the whilst?

York. As in a theater the eyes of men,
After a well-graced actor leaves the stage,
Are idly bent on him that enters next,
Thinking his prattle to be tedious;
Even so, or with much more contempt, men's eyes
Did scowl on gentle Richard; no man cried "God save him!"
No joyful tongue gave him his welcome home,
But dust was thrown upon his sacred head;
Which with such gentle sorrow he shook off,
His face still combating with tears and smiles,
The badges of his grief and patience,
That had not God for some strong purpose steeled
The hearts of men, they must perforce have melted,

And barbarism itself have pitied him.

But heaven hath a hand in these events,

To whose high will we bound our calm contents.

To Bolingbroke are we sworn subjects now,

Whose state and honor I for aye allow.

    [Enter Aumerle].

Duchess. Here comes my son, Aumerle.

York.   Aumerle that was,

But that is lost for being Richard's friend;

And, madam, you must call him Rutland now.

I am in Parliament pledge for his truth

And lasting fealty to the new-made king.

Duchess. Welcome, my son; who are the violets now

That strew the green lap of the new-come spring?

Aumerle. Madam, I know not, nor I greatly care not.

God knows I had as lief be none as one.

York. Well, bear you well in this new spring of time,

Lest you be cropped before you come to prime.

What news from Oxford? Do these jousts and triumphs hold?

Aumerle. For aught I know, my lord, they do.

York. You will be there, I know.

Aumerle. If God prevent me not, I purpose so.

York. What seal is that that hangs without thy bosom?

Yea, look'st thou pale? Let me see the writing.

Aumerle. My lord, 'tis nothing.

York. No matter, then, who see it.

I will be satisfied: let me see the writing.

Aumerle. I do beseech your Grace to pardon me:

It is a matter of small consequence,

Which for some reasons I would not have seen.

York. Which for some reasons, sir, I mean to see.

I fear, I fear—

Duchess.   What should you fear?

        'Tis nothing but some band that he is ent'red into

        For gay apparel 'gainst the triumph day.

York.   Bound to himself? What doth he with a bond

        That he is bound to? Wife, thou art a fool.

        Boy, let me see the writing.

Aumerle.   I do beseech you, pardon me. I may not show it.

York.   I will be satisfied. Let me see it, I say!

            [*He plucks it out of his bosom and reads it*]

        Treason, foul treason, villain, traitor, slave!

Duchess.   What is the matter, my lord?

York.   Ho, who is within there? Saddle my horse.

        God for his mercy! What treachery is here!

Duchess.   Why, what is it, my lord?

York.   Give me my boots, I say! Saddle my horse!

        Now, by mine honor, by my life, my troth,

        I will appeach the villain.

Duchess.   What is the matter?

York.	Peace, foolish woman.
Duchess.	I will not peace. What is the matter, Aumerle?
Aumerle.	Good mother, be content; it is no more
	Than my poor life must answer.
Duchess.	Thy life answer?
York.	Bring me my boots: I will unto the King.
	[*His man enters with his boots*]
Duchess.	Strike him, Aumerle. Poor boy, thou art amazed.
	Hence, villain, never more come in my sight.
York.	Give me my boots, I say.
Duchess.	Why, York, what wilt thou do?
	Wilt thou not hide the trespass of thine own?
	Have we more sons? Or are we like to have?
	Is not my teeming date drunk up with time?
	And wilt thou pluck my fair son from mine age?
	And rob me of a happy mother's name?
	Is he not like thee? Is he not thine own?

York.   Thou fond, mad woman,
Wilt thou conceal this dark conspiracy?
A dozen of them here have ta'en the sacrament
And interchangeably set down their hands
To kill the King at Oxford.

Duchess.   He shall be none;
We'll keep him here. Then what is that to him?

York.   Away, fond woman, were he twenty times my son,
I would appeach him.

Duchess.   Had'st thou groaned for him
As I have done, thou would'st be more pitiful.
But now I know thy mind; thou dost suspect
That I have been disloyal to thy bed,
And that he is a bastard, not thy son:
Sweet York, sweet husband, be not of that mind;
He is as like thee as a man may be,
Not like to me, or any of my kin,
And yet I love him.

York. Make way, unruly woman.

[*Exit*]

Duchess. After, Aumerle! Mount thee upon his horse;

Spur, post, and get before him to the King,

And beg thy pardon ere he do accuse thee.

I'll not be long behind; though I be old,

I doubt not but to ride as fast as York;

And never will I rise up from the ground

Till Bolingbroke have pardoned thee. Away! Be gone!

[*Exeunt*]

SCENE III
WINDSOR CASTLE

*[Enter Bolingbroke, now the King,
with his Nobles, Percy and others]*

Bolingbroke.   Can no man tell me of my unthrifty son?
'Tis full three months since I did see him last.
If any plague hang over us, 'tis he.
I would to God, my lords, he might be found:
Inquire at London, 'mongst the taverns there,
For there, they say, he daily doth frequent
With unrestrainèd loose companions,
Even such, they say, as stand in narrow lanes,
And beat our watch and rob our passengers;
While he, young wanton and effeminate boy,
Takes on the point of honor to support
So dissolute a crew.

Percy. My lord, some two days since I saw the Prince,

And told him of those triumphs held at Oxford.

Bolingbroke. And what said the gallant?

Percy. His answer was, he would unto the stews,

And from the commonest creature pluck a glove,

And wear it as a favor, and with that

He would unhorse the lustiest challenger.

Bolingbroke. As dissolute as desperate; but yet

Through both I see some sparks of better hope,

Which elder years may happily bring forth.

But who comes here?

[*Enter Aumerle, amazed*]

Aumerle. Where is the King?

Bolingbroke. What means

Our cousin, that he stares and looks so wildly?

Aumerle. God save your Grace! I do beseech your Majesty

To have some conference with your Grace alone.

Bolingbroke. Withdraw yourselves, and leave us here alone.

[*Exeunt Percy and Lords*]

What is the matter with our cousin now?

Aumerle.	For ever may my knees grow to the earth, *[Kneels]* My tongue cleave to my roof within my mouth, Unless a pardon ere I rise or speak.
Bolingbroke.	Intended, or committed, was this fault? If on the first, how heinous e'er it be, To win thy after-love I pardon thee.
Aumerle.	Then give me leave that I may turn the key, That no man enter till my tale be done.

Bolingbroke.	Have thy desire.
	    [Aumerle locks the door. The Duke of
	    York knocks at the door and crieth]

York.	*[Within]* My liege, beware, look to thyself: Thou hast a traitor in thy presence there.
Bolingbroke.	Villain, I'll make thee safe. *[Draws his sword]*
Aumerle.	Stay thy revengeful hand; thou hast no cause to fear.

York.　Open the door, secure, foolhardy King!

Shall I for love speak treason to thy face?

Open the door, or I will break it open.

　　　[*Bolingbroke opens*]

　　　[*Enter York*]

Bolingbroke.　What is the matter, uncle? Speak.

　　　[*He relocks door*]

Recover breath. Tell us, how near is danger,

That we may arm us to encounter it.

York.　Peruse this writing here, and thou shalt know

The treason that my haste forbids me show.

Aumerle.　Remember, as thou read'st, thy promise passed.

I do repent me, read not my name there;

My heart is not confederate with my hand.

York.　It was, villain, ere thy hand did set it down.

I tore it from the traitor's bosom, King:

Fear, and not love, begets his penitence.

Forget to pity him, lest thy pity prove

A serpent that will sting thee to the heart.

Bolingbroke.   O heinous, strong and bold conspiracy!

O loyal father of a treacherous son!

Thou sheer immaculate and silver fountain,

From whence this stream, through muddy passages,

Hath held his current, and defiled himself,

Thy overflow of good converts to bad;

And thy abundant goodness shall excuse

This deadly blot in thy digressing son.

York.   So shall my virtue be his vice's bawd,

And he shall spend mine honor with his shame,

As thriftless sons their scraping fathers' gold.

Mine honor lives when his dishonor dies,

Or my shamed life in his dishonor lies.

Thou kill'st me in his life, giving him breath;

The traitor lives, the true man's put to death.

Duchess.	[*Within*] What ho! My liege, for God's sake, let me in!
Bolingbroke.	What shrill-voiced suppliant makes this eager cry?
Duchess.	A woman, and thy aunt, great King—'tis I.
	Speak with me, pity me, open the door;
	A beggar begs that never begged before.
Bolingbroke.	Our scene is alt'red from a serious thing,
	And now changed to "The Beggar and the King."
	My dangerous cousin, let your mother in:
	I know she is come to pray for your foul sin.

       [*Aumerle unlocks door during York's speech*]

York.	If thou do pardon, whosoever pray,
	More sins for this forgiveness prosper may.

       [*Enter Duchess*]

This fest'red joint cut off, the rest rest sound;

This let alone will all the rest confound.

Duchess. O King, believe not this hardhearted man:

Love loving not itself, none other can.

York. Thou frantic woman, what dost thou make here?

Shall thy old dugs once more a traitor rear?

Duchess. Sweet York, be patient. Hear me, gentle liege.

    [Kneels]

Bolingbroke. Rise up, good aunt.

Duchess.   Not yet, I thee beseech.

For ever will I walk upon my knees,

And never see day that the happy sees,

Till thou give joy—until thou bid me joy—

By pardoning Rutland, my transgressing boy.

Aumerle. Unto my mother's prayers I bend my knee.

    [Kneels]

York. Against them both my true joints bended be;

    [Kneels]

Ill may'st thou thrive, if thou grant any grace.

Duchess.   Pleads he in earnest? Look upon his face.

His eyes do drop no tears, his prayers are in jest;

His words come from his mouth, ours from our breast;

He prays but faintly, and would be denied;

We pray with heart and soul, and all beside;

His weary joints would gladly rise, I know;

Our knees still kneel till to the ground they grow;

His prayers are full of false hypocrisy,

Ours of true zeal and deep integrity;

Our prayers do outpray his—then let them have

That mercy which true prayer ought to have.

Bolingbroke.   Good aunt, stand up.

Duchess.   Nay, do not say "Stand up";

Say "Pardon" first, and afterwards "Stand up";

And if I were thy nurse thy tongue to teach,

"Pardon" should be the first word of thy speech.

I never longed to hear a word till now.

Say "Pardon," King; let pity teach thee how.

The word is short, but not so short as sweet:

No word like "pardon" for kings' mouths so meet.

York.	Speak it in French, King; say "Pardonne moy."
Duchess.	Dost thou teach pardon pardon to destroy?
	Ah, my sour husband, my hardhearted lord!
	That sets the word itself against the word.
	Speak "Pardon" as 'tis current in our land:
	The chopping French we do not understand.
	Thine eye begins to speak; set thy tongue there,
	Or in thy piteous heart plant thou thine ear,
	That hearing how our plaints and prayers do pierce,
	Pity may move thee "Pardon" to rehearse.
Bolingbroke.	Good aunt, stand up.
Duchess.	I do not sue to stand.
	Pardon is all the suit I have in hand.
Bolingbroke.	I pardon him as God shall pardon me.
Duchess.	O, happy vantage of a kneeling knee!
	Yet am I sick for fear; speak it again.
	Twice saying "Pardon" doth not pardon twain,
	But makes one pardon strong.

Bolingbroke.   With all my heart

I pardon him.

Duchess.   A god on earth thou art.

                   [*York and Aumerle rise*]

Bolingbroke.   But for our trusty brother-in-law, and the abbot,

With all the rest of that consorted crew,

Destruction straight shall dog them at the heels.

Good uncle, help to order several powers

To Oxford, or where'er these traitors are;

They shall not live within this world, I swear,

But I will have them if I once know where.

Uncle, farewell, and cousin, too, adieu.

Your mother well hath prayed, and prove you true.

Duchess.   Come, my old son, I pray God make thee new.

                   [*Exeunt*]

SCENE IV
WINDSOR CASTLE

[Enter Sir Pierce Exton & a Man]

Exton.   Didst thou not mark the King, what words he spake?

          "Have I no friend will rid me of this living fear?"

          Was it not so?

Man.   These were his very words.

Exton. "Have I no friend?" quoth he: he spake it twice,

          And urged it twice together, did he not?

Man.   He did.

Exton.   And speaking it, he wishtly looked on me,

          As who should say, "I would thou wert the man

          That would divorce this terror from my heart"—

          Meaning the King at Pomfret. Come, let's go:

          I am the King's friend, and will rid his foe.

        [Exeunt]

[*Enter Richard alone*]

Richard.   I have been studying how I may compare

This prison where I live unto the world:

And for because the world is populous,

And here is not a creature but myself,

I cannot do it. Yet I'll hammer it out:

My brain I'll prove the female to my soul,

My soul the father, and these two beget

A generation of still-breeding thoughts;

And these same thoughts people this little world,

In humors like the people of this world,

For no thought is contented. The better sort,

As thoughts of things divine are intermixed

With scruples, and do set the word itself

Against the word; as thus: "Come, little ones";

And then again,

"It is as hard to come as for a camel
    To thread the postern of a small needle's eye."
Thoughts tending to ambition, they do plot
Unlikely wonders: how these vain weak nails
May tear a passage through the flinty ribs
Of this hard world, my ragged prison walls;
And, for they cannot, die in their own pride.
Thoughts tending to content flatter themselves
That they are not the first of fortune's slaves,
Nor shall not be the last, like seely beggars
Who sitting in the stocks refuge their shame,
That many have, and others must, sit there;
And in this thought they find a kind of ease,
Bearing their own misfortunes on the back
Of such as have endured the like.
Thus play I in one person many people,
And none contented; sometimes am I king,
Then treasons make me wish myself a beggar,
And so I am. Then crushing penury

Persuades me I was better when a king.

Then am I kinged again and, by and by,

Think that I am unkinged by Bolingbroke,

And straight am nothing. But whate'er I be,

Nor I, nor any man that but man is,

With nothing shall be pleased, till he be eased

With being nothing.

      [The music plays]

                   Music do I hear.

Ha—ha! Keep time! How sour sweet music is

When time is broke, and no proportion kept;

So is it in the music of men's lives:

And here have I the daintiness of ear

To check time broke in a disordered string,

But for the concord of my state and time,

Had not an ear to hear my true time broke.

I wasted time, and now doth Time waste me:

For now hath Time made me his numb'ring clock;

My thoughts are minutes, and with sighs they jar

Their watches on unto mine eyes, the outward watch
Whereto my finger, like a dial's point,
Is pointing still, in cleansing them from tears.
Now, sir, the sound that tells what hour it is
Are clamorous groans which strike upon my heart,
Which is the bell. So sighs, and tears, and groans,
Show minutes, times, and hours; but my time
Runs posting on in Bolingbroke's proud joy,
While I stand fooling here, his Jack-of-the-clock.
This music mads me: let it sound no more.
For though it have holp madmen to their wits,
In me it seems it will make wise men mad.
Yet blessing on his heart that gives it me,
For 'tis a sign of love; and love to Richard
Is a strange brooch in this all-hating world.
  [*Enter a Groom of the stable*]

Groom. Hail, royal Prince!

Richard.   Thanks, noble peer!

The cheapest of us is ten groats too dear.

What art thou? And how comest thou hither,

Where no man ever comes, but that sad dog

That brings me food to make misfortune live?

Groom. I was a poor groom of thy stable, King,

When thou wert King, who, traveling towards York,

With much ado at length have gotten leave

To look upon my sometimes royal master's face.

O, how it ern'd my heart, when I beheld

In London streets, that coronation day,

When Bolingbroke rode on roan Barbary,

That horse that thou so often hast bestrid,

That horse that I so carefully have dressed.

Richard.	Rode he on Barbary? Tell me, gentle friend,
	How went he under him?
Groom.	So proudly as if he disdained the ground.
Richard.	So proud that Bolingbroke was on his back!
	That jade hath eat bread from my royal hand;
	This hand hath made him proud with clapping him.
	Would he not stumble? Would he not fall down,
	Since pride must have a fall, and break the neck
	Of that proud man that did usurp his back?
	Forgiveness, horse! Why do I rail on thee,
	Since thou created to be awed by man
	Wast born to bear? I was not made a horse,
	And yet I bear a burden like an ass,
	Spurred, galled, and tired by jauncing Bolingbroke.

{Enter a Keeper, with meat for Richard}

Keeper. Fellow, give place; here is no longer stay.

Richard. If thou love me, 'tis time thou wert away.

Groom. What my tongue dares not, that my heart shall say.

      [Exit Groom]

Keeper. My lord, wilt please you to fall to?

Richard. Taste of it first, as thou art wont to do.

Keeper. My lord, I dare not; Sir Pierce of Exton

      Who lately came from the King, commands the contrary.

Richard. The devil take Henry of Lancaster, and thee!

      Patience is stale, and I am weary of it.

Keeper. Help, help, help!

      [The murderers, Exton and Servants, rush in]

Richard. How now! What means Death in this rude assault?

Villain, thy own hand yields thy death's instrument.

  [*Snatches a weapon and kills one*]

Go thou, and fill another room in hell!

  [*He kills another. Here Exton strikes him down*]

That hand shall burn in never-quenching fire

That staggers thus my person. Exton, thy fierce hand

Hath with the King's blood stained the King's own land.

Mount, mount, my soul; thy seat is up on high,

Whilst my gross flesh sinks downward here to die.

  [*Dies*]

Exton. As full of valor as of royal blood!

Both have I spilled. O, would the deed were good!

For now the devil that told me I did well

Says that this deed is chronicled in hell.

This dead king to the living king I'll bear.

Take hence the rest, and give them burial here.

  [*Exeunt with the bodies*]

SCENE VI

WINDSOR CASTLE

*[Flourish. Enter Bolingbroke with the Duke
of York, and other Lords and Attendants]*

Bolingbroke.   Kind uncle York, the latest news we hear

Is that the rebels have consumed with fire

Our town of Ciceter in Gloucestershire,

But whether they be ta'en or slain we hear not.

    [Enter Northumberland]

Welcome, my lord; what is the news?

Northumberland.   First, to thy sacred state wish I all happiness;

The next news is, I have to London sent

The heads of Salisbury, Spencer, Blunt, and Kent.

The manner of their taking may appear

At large discoursèd in this paper here.

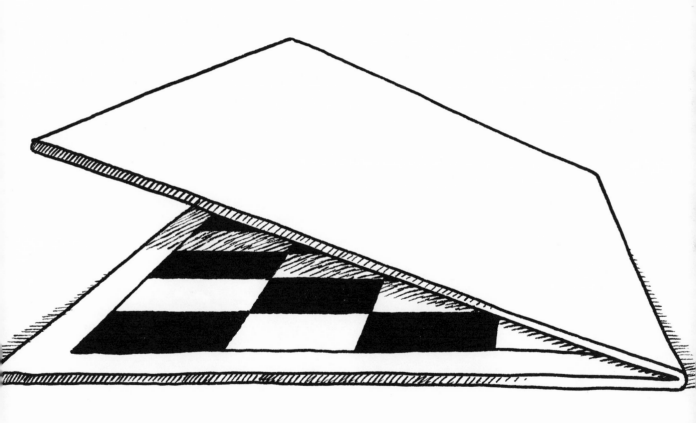

Bolingbroke.	We thank thee, gentle Percy, for thy pains,
	And to thy worth will add right worthy gains.

[Enter Lord Fitzwater]

Fitzwater.	My lord, I have from Oxford sent to London
	The heads of Brocas and Sir Bennet Seely,
	Two of the dangerous consorted traitors
	That sought at Oxford thy dire overthrow.
Bolingbroke.	Thy pains, Fitzwater, shall not be forgot:
	Right noble is thy merit well I wot.

[Enter Henry Percy and the Bishop of Carlisle]

Percy.	The grand conspirator, Abbot of Westminster,
	With clog of conscience and sour meloncholy,
	Hath yielded up his body to the grave;
	But here is Carlisle living, to abide
	Thy kingly doom, and sentence of his pride.

Bolingbroke. Carlisle, this is your doom:

Choose out some secret place, some reverend room

More than thou hast, and with it joy thy life.

So as thou liv'st in peace, die free from strife;

For though mine enemy thou hast ever been,

High sparks of honor in thee have I seen.

[Enter Exton with Attendants bearing the coffin]

Exton. Great King, within this coffin I present

Thy buried fear: herein all breathless lies

The mightiest of thy greatest enemies,

Richard of Bordeaux, by me hither brought.

Bolingbroke. Exton, I thank thee not, for thou hast wrought

A deed of slander with thy fatal hand

Upon my head and all this famous land.

Exton. From your own mouth, my lord, did I this deed.

Bolingbroke.   They love not poison that do poison need,

Nor do I thee; though I did wish him dead,

I hate the murderer, love him murderèd.

The guilt of conscience take thou for thy labor,

But neither my good word, nor princely favor.

With Cain go wander thorough shades of night,

And never show thy head by day nor light.

　　　[*Exit Exton*]

Lords, I protest, my soul is full of woe,

That blood should sprinkle me to make me grow.

Come, mourn with me for what I do lament,

And put on sullen black incontinent.

I'll make a voyage to the Holy Land,

To wash this blood off from my guilty hand.

March sadly after; grace my mournings here,

In weeping after this untimely bier.

　　　[*Exeunt*]

FINIS

COLOPHON

Typography by the ComposingRoom inc.
The text was set in 14 pt. Linotype Janson, 8 pt. leaded
with 11 pt. Italics. The display copy is Photo Display Janson.
Complete page negatives were prepared for platemaking.
Printed Lithography by Rae Publishing Co., Inc. The paper,
manufactured by Finch, Pruyn & Company, Inc., is Finch Textbook
Offset, Vellum Finish, Cream White, Basis 80, 312 pages per inch.
Binding by A. Horowitz & Son/Bookbinders, with Kingston
Natural Finish 35369. Endpapers are Elephant hide No. 19.
Typographic coordination by Irving Levine.
Illustrations are by Isadore Seltzer.
Design by Daniel Haberman.

WILLIAM SHAKESPEARE:

THE TRAGEDY OF KING RICHARD II